Withdrawn

the mystery of arafat

DANNY RUBINSTEIN

TRANSLATED BY DAN LEON

STEERFORTH PRESS
SOUTH ROYALTON, VERMONT

For information about permission to reproduce selections
from this book, write to: Steerforth Press L.C., P.O. Box 70,
South Royalton, Vermont 05068.

Library of Congress Cataloging-in-Publication Data
Rubinstein, Danny.
The mystery of Arafat / by Danny Rubinstein.
p.   cm.
ISBN 1–883642–10–8
1. Arafat, Yasir,—1929– —Psychology.   2. Munazzamat al-Tahrir
al-Filastiniyah—Biography.   3. Palestinian Arabs—Biography.
4. Jewish-Arab relations—1949–   5. Israel-Arab conflicts.   I. Title.
DS119.7.A6785R83   1995
956.D4 092—dc20   95–9748

Manufactured in the United States of America

First Edition

contents

chronology

August 1929: Yasser Arafat was born, a little more than ten years after the British Mandate in Palestine had begun, and the Ottoman Empire's four-hundred-year control of the Arab Middle East had ended. Arafat's father was a lower middle-class merchant in Gaza, and his mother the daughter of an old Jerusalem family.

1947: Arafat completed high school in Cairo, Egypt, where he had spent his childhood and teenage years. In November 1947 the General Assembly of the United Nations made the resolution to partition Palestine between the Jewish and Arab communities. The Arabs rejected the resolution and war broke out in the land.

1948: Yasser Arafat began to study engineering at Cairo University early in the year. In the spring he volunteered to go to Palestine and take part in the fighting. On 15 May 1948, the British Mandate came to an end, and David Ben-Gurion announced the creation of the State of Israel. The armies of seven Arab states invaded Palestine in order to prevent the establishment of the Jewish state.

1949: Arafat returned to Cairo to continue his studies. The war between Israel and the Arab states ended with an Israeli victory and the signing of an armistice with the neighboring Arab countries. As a result of the war, Israel controlled two-thirds of Palestine.

Half of the 1.3 million Palestinian Arabs became refugees. Jordan annexed the western hills of Judea and Samaria, which came to be known as the West Bank. A narrow strip on the southern seashore of Palestine came under Egyptian military rule and was called the Gaza Strip.

1950–1956: Arafat completed his engineering studies, devoting most of his time to political student activities as chairman of the Palestinian student organization at the university.

November 1956: Israel, coordinated with France and Britain, moved militarily toward the Suez Canal in response to Egyptian President Gamal Abdel Nasser's nationalization of the Canal. Israel occupied the Sinai Peninsula, but was forced to withdraw under American and Soviet ultimatum.

1957: Arafat left Egypt and got a job as an engineer in Kuwait. Together with other young Palestinian activists, established a small organization named al-Fatah.

1964: a number of veteran Palestinian activists, led by Ahmed Shukairy, established the Palestine Liberation Organization (PLO), under the auspices of the Egyptian regime. Arafat and his colleagues were not part of the new Palestinian movement.

1965: Arafat's Fatah launched the first military operation against Israel. The action provoked a stormy response in the Arab world and in Israel, and helped to fuel animosities which would lead to 1967's Six-Day War.

June 1967: Egyptian provocation sparked the Six-Day War, and an intense Israeli air strike led to Israel's victory. At the end of six days, Israel was in control of the Jordanian West Bank, the Egyptian Gaza Strip and Sinai Peninsula, and the Syrian Golan Heights. The Palestinian population of the West Bank and Gaza came under Israeli military government. After the war, Arafat and Fatah escalated their attacks against Israel, and other radical Palestinian groups joined them. They adopted a military strategy similar to the one which had earned Algeria its independence, and which included terrorist activity against Israel's civilian population.

March 1968: Israel launched an attack on the headquarters of the Palestinian organizations, located in the town of Karameh, east of the Jordan river. After a day-long fight, the Israeli army withdrew, and the Palestinians declared victory.

1969: Arafat and his people took control of the PLO, and Arafat was chosen to be its chairman.

1970: Jordan's army attempted to stop Palestinian operations along its eastern border with Israel. The Palestinians posed a challenge to Jordanian sovereignty, and in essence were creating a state within a state.

Summer of 1970: after Palestinians hijacked passenger planes and forced them to land in Jordan, a civil war broke out in which King Hussein attempted to crush the PLO structure in the kingdom. After the bloody civil war (known as Black September), Arafat and the Palestinian activists withdrew from Jordan to Lebanon.

October 1973: Egypt and Syria initiated a surprise attack against Israel, which was followed by political negotiations. Arafat and the PLO revealed the first signs that they would be willing to use political means in addition to military and terrorist activities in order to achieve their goals.

November 1974: Arafat was invited to speak before the United Nations General Assembly. The Arab world recognized the PLO as the sole representative of the Palestinian people.

Late 1977: President Anwar Sadat of Egypt made a dramatic visit to Jerusalem, which led to negotiations and a separate peace treaty between Israel and Egypt. Arafat and the majority of the Arab leaders rejected the treaty.

June 1982: Israel attacked PLO bases in Lebanon, putting Beirut under siege, and forced Arafat to evacuate Lebanon. Most of the PLO administration moved to Tunis.

December 1987: a popular uprising known as the Intifada started in the West Bank and Gaza. PLO grass roots organizers played a major role in leading the uprising. However, under Arafat's guidance, the PLO gradually moved its followers toward political, instead of military, resistance.

November 1988: the PLO made the decision to accept the UN resolution which called for the recognition of Israel and the renunciation of terrorism.

1991: after the Gulf War caused a schism in the Arab world, an international conference in Madrid marked the opening of a comprehensive peace process between Israel and much of the Arab world. Though the PLO was not formally represented in Madrid, a Palestinian delegation comprised of leaders from the occupied territories who were known to have been selected by the PLO leadership did participate. The conference set a precedent by arranging the first direct talks between Israel and the Palestinians.

1993: secret talks in Oslo between the Israeli Labor Party government and Arafat's emissaries led to an agreement that mutual recognition and the establishment of a Palestinian authority in Gaza and Jericho would comprise the first steps to a final agreement, later signed in Washington.

Summer of 1994: Arafat arrived in Gaza and established the first Palestinian government in Palestine.

December 1994: Arafat shared the Nobel Peace Prize with Israeli Prime Minister Yitzhak Shamir and Foreign Minister Shimon Peres.

foreword

For the last 28 years, I have written the name Yasser Arafat almost every day. I am an Israeli journalist, and have been writing on Arab and Palestinian affairs since 1967. I have met Yasser Arafat on a number of occasions; in 1993, at the time of the then-secret Israeli-PLO negotiations, we met in Tunis and engaged in a conversation which lasted several hours. I have read a vast amount of material about him: books, works of research, documents, and current press reports. Over the course of years I have held or heard innumerable conversations on the subject of Arafat and I have imagined that I knew him well.

It is doubtful, though, whether anyone can make that claim. In my meetings with Palestinians, when his name invariably comes up, I hear again and again that they, his own people, are baffled in their attempts to analyze his character, interpret his actions, and prophesy his behavior. Some profess boundless admiration for him, others are confounded by his shallowness and ignorance. I hear people gossip about him, joke at his expense, denigrate him, and of course praise and glorify his name. In many of my meetings with Israelis, Arabs, Americans, and others, serious efforts are made to understand the man and his character. While some speak of him with disgust and others with appreciation, most are above all perplexed over this strange phenomenon called Yasser Arafat.

A massive quantity of material was thus at my disposal when I undertook to write this book, but this vast amount of information did nothing to make the job any easier. Arafat's underground military and political activities have created a paradoxical situation: on the one hand reams of material about him have been produced for public consumption, while on the other hand, he and his associates have carefully emphasized the mystery and secrecy surrounding him. For years Arafat demonstrated this emphasis by wearing dark glasses even during indoor meetings. How enigmatic they made him look, and yet when asked why he wore them, he simply replied so that nobody would know if he were awake or dozing.[1]

The bitter differences over the Middle Eastern conflict created a situation in which most reports about Arafat have been colored by the reporter's personal opinions. To appreciate this one need only glance at the titles he is given. Most writers call him "the PLO leader" or "the Chairman of the PLO Executive." In Palestinian publications after 1988 he is "the President of Palestine"— a title he received with the symbolic declaration of Palestinian independence at the PLO Council meeting in Algeria. Since arriving in Gaza, he has become "the Chairman of the Palestinan Authority." Outside the Middle East, Arafat has for years been called "the head of the Palestinian guerrilla organizations" while among the Israelis he has simply been described as "head of the PLO terrorist organization."

Each of these descriptions carries significance, and sometimes the choice of Arafat's title is in itself enough to indicate whether the reporter is sympathetic or hostile. It is almost impossible to remain neutral concerning Arafat. There is at least one biography which slanders him and two others which extol him.[2] In this book I have tried as far as possible to preserve a balanced attitude, avoiding either any glorification or any denigration of his name and work. It seems to me that the impression Arafat makes has always been more important than what he really is. His principle role has been to serve as a symbol. Accordingly, this is not a condensed biography but an attempt to examine Arafat's image, both from media reports and research and from what emerges in chance conversations in the Palestinian street. In my view, Arafat's importance as a historical figure will be determined more than anything by the extent to which his image has had an impact or value vis-à-vis major events in the Middle East. Therefore, if any political stand or personal bias of my own emerges from between the lines of this book, it is unintentional.

The examination of a myth or a symbol can always be construed as an impulse to smash idols or to slaughter sacred cows. I have tried to avoid this. I have found that Palestinian writers and researchers have hardly dealt with Arafat's mythic aspect, perhaps out of fear that they would be unable to preserve the necessary distance when observing the man and his life's work. In a similar vein, my problem as an Israeli writer stems from Arafat's strong image as an enemy. I have tried, therefore, to strike a balance among what I have heard and read from Palestinians, Arabs, Israelis, and foreign sources.

I was beset in writing this book by a sense of bewilderment which I have felt for many years regarding Arafat's enigmatic personality. To a large extent my writing was actuated by personal curiosity and the desire to understand what at first sight appeared to be strange and incomprehensible. I first described the problem and then went from stage to stage in an attempt to answer it. The stages include all those details which I considered relevant in Arafat's life, political action and theory, personal bahavior, character, way of life, and faith. It is these which together make up the overall picture of Arafat's personality, and its political significance. What follows is like unraveling a riddle—an attempt to lay bare the seemingly mysterious and paradoxical character of Yasser Arafat.

Danny Rubinstein
Jerusalem
December 1994

the enigma of yasser arafat

"All eyes are turned on Yasser Arafat, for he is both the problem and the solution."
                —From the introduction to an interview with him
                    by Ibrahim al-Barjawi, Amin al-Sibai, and Zaki
                        Shihab, *Al-Hawadeth,* Beirut, 8 January 1982.

He is one of this half century's best-known personalities. Five comprehensive biographies have been written about him and he has been a principal figure in hundreds of other books. For years his image has been a permanent feature on television newscasts throughout the world. Not a week passes without interviews with him in internationally read newspapers and magazines. He is "Mr. Palestine," recipient along with the Israeli leaders of the highest international honor, the Nobel Peace Prize.

Yet the man who for decades has personified the Palestinian problem and its solution has, in the eyes of many, been a laughable and often offensive figure. What epithets have not been used to describe Arafat: unscrupulous, unreliable, capricious, untrustworthy. Despite all this, his leadership has almost miraculously survived. Although throughout his career he has lacked the mechanisms of state sovereignty with which to accumulate power and exert authority, he is the sole leader of his people. He behaves

with ridiculous theatricality and speaks such poor Arabic that
a professor of Arabic in East Jerusalem once joked that Arafat's
English was better than his Arabic. One is bound to wonder—
isn't there anyone in the Palestinian leadership more capable than
this man?

The vast majority of Israelis don't trust Arafat, first and foremost
because they fear that he has not changed his past adherence to
what the Palestinians called "armed struggle" and what the Israelis
see merely as murderous terror. Many Israelis are certain that it
was only for ulterior motives that Arafat retreated from the original Palestinian ideology which demanded the elimination of the
state of Israel.

One of Arafat's Israeli acquaintances, the journalist and former
Knesset member Uri Avneri, once said that nobody has been
hated in Israel as much as Arafat and "it appears that a hundred
years of enmity, hatred and fear are channeled into the Israeli attitude toward him. He has been called, among other things, an Arab
Hitler, a bloodthirsty terrorist,[3] corrupt, an embezzler, a sexual
deviant, a swindler, a coward." Recently, following the agreement
with Israel, he has been seen as "a harbinger of chaos, a madman,
a dictator."

This impression is confirmed for Israelis by various assertions
Arafat has made which, though they might seem insignificant,
disqualify him in their eyes from serving as a credible partner for
dialogue. How is one to take Arafat after his declarations in dozens
of interviews that the emblem hung up over the entry to the
Knesset in Jerusalem is a map depicting Eretz Yisrael (Palestine) as
stretching from the Nile to the Euphrates? "For many years (this
emblem) has flown over the main entrance to the Knesset, their
Parliament," said Arafat in an interview with *Playboy* in August
1988 and with *Jeune Afrique* in August 1987.

The facts in this matter are quite simple. Millions of visitors
have come to the Israeli Knesset, passed through its entrances and

examined them. There has never been an emblem or map of this nature. Many people, including associates and confidants of Arafat, must have told him that there was no truth in the story. Yet for one reason or another, he has repeated it again and again, using it as a symbol of that Israeli expansionism which has both injured his people and served his political purposes.

In speeches and public appearances he has also claimed to see the Nile and the Euphrates rivers in the two blue lines on the Israeli flag.[4] On several occasions he has referred as well to the Israeli ten-agorot coin on which there appears a menorah (candelabrum) against the background of a stain which he says depicts the borders for which Israel strives, again from Egypt to Iraq. No Israeli, even those sympathetic with the Palestinian situation, can accept such fatuous and preposterous interpretations. The lines on the Zionist flag were designed according to the tallith (prayer shawl) while the stain on the coin was copied from the remnants of an ancient Israeli coin. These symbols have nothing whatsoever to do with Israel's borders (which some Israelis would indeed like to expand). Can a serious leader possibly hark back again and again to such nonsense?

If Arafat is a leader of stature, Israelis ask, why upon his arrival in Gaza and Jericho in July 1994 to lay the foundations for the Palestinian State, did he confer on Rabbi Moshe Hirsch the nebulous title of minister in the Palestinian government, responsible for "Jewish affairs." Hirsch is well-known in the Israeli media as a clownish figure who comes from the most marginal periphery of Jerusalem's anti-Zionist ultra-orthodox rabbinical circles. Publicity-mad and without any following, he harasses journalists in their offices or from a phone booth near his home. Israelis consider him at best a poor joke—yet here was Arafat hugging and kissing him at the ceremony which celebrated his return, proudly posing for photographs with him and even granting him meaningless office as a member of the first Palestinian Cabinet. It is on the basis of this sort of behavior that Israeli Foreign Minister Shimon Peres once said, "Yasser Arafat is amazing both in his wisdom and in his stupidity."[5]

Not only in Israel but also in the West, in Europe and in the United States, people are perplexed by the Arafat enigma. With his terrorist image clearly remembered, he is placed somewhere among those strange Third World despots who still hold out against democratic freedoms and international law. His refusal to remove his gun belt when addressing the United Nations in 1974 is not forgotten. His outward appearance and exhibitionist behavior, as well as the public scandals he has created, have repelled many people. For example, in Cairo he broke the rules of protocol by publicly refusing, for no apparent reason, to sign some of the documents of the PLO aggreement with Israel (May 1994).

Nor is his supportive embrace of Saddam Hussein on the eve of the Gulf War easily forgotten. Why did he join up with the brutal and aggressive ruler in Baghdad when nearly the whole world was united against him? When I asked him in his Tunis office in the spring of 1993 why he had supported Saddam Hussein, he feigned innocence and tried to deny it: "Why should I suddenly have supported him? It's not true"—as if nobody had seen or heard him during the crisis.

And yet Arafat's great political importance has been universally recognized. He has been written about in superlatives: "Without doubt one of the most unusual characters and unlikely statesmen ever to grace the world stage," writes journalist Thomas Friedman, who reported on him from the Middle East for ten years. "Arafat's great achievement was that he led the Palestinians out of the deserts of obscurity into the land of prime time ... galvanized them into a coherent and internationally recognized national liberation movement, and transformed them in the eyes of the world from refugees in need of tents to a nation in need of sovereignty."[6]

Nor has Arafat's path been easy. In his quest for a Palestinian state, he has had to work in nearly impossible conditions. From the beginning of his activity in the early 1950s he has had to struggle not only against Israel, but also against the Arab peoples, the United States, and most of the West. Against the strong and well-equipped Israeli army Arafat has had to pitch groups of youngsters who from a military point of view lacked any prospects whatsoever.

But far more important than the hopeless military conflict was the moral-political struggle which the Palestinians waged under Arafat. In the wake of the holocaust which destroyed a third of the Jewish people, the Jewish state possessed powerful moral superiority. Holocaust survivors, who were fighting for the right to that piece of land where their historical heritage originated, gained wide sympathy in international public opinion. Arafat challenged this moral superiority and to a large extent overcame it. He exploited to the utmost international and regional political circumstances, and especially Israeli rule since 1967 over the West Bank and Gaza Strip, and perhaps it was in this area that he gained his most impressive achievement.

Among his own people and even within his entourage, there are nonetheless many who dislike Arafat. It is hard to stomach his outbursts of anger accompanied by crude curses, and the trickery and manipulations practiced not only on his opponents but also on his associates. Exact quotes of harsh words to those within his own circles are hard to come by, but at least once, his words on the telephone to the PLO representative in Paris, Ibrahim Sus, were recorded (January 1992). This was after Sus had informed him that Jewish pressure had prevented the French government from providing Palestinian opposition leader George Habash with medical treatment. Arafat burst out: "The Jews are at work. Curse their fathers, dogs, filth, scum, all because of a sick person. I looked after their sick POWs, but trash remains trash." The taped conversation was broadcast on CNN, with the voices of the speakers, Arafat and Sus, easily recognizable.[7]

Arafat has often been described as lacking in personal charisma.[8] His has never been a magnetic personality and people never emerge from meetings with him overwhelmed by emotion. Since he is recognized as a leader, he naturally has had all the symbols of status: bodyguards, an entourage of associates and assistants and official cars, but even those around him do not always treat him with respect. Like many who have interviewed him for a period of hours, I have noticed that his assistants and advisors will often stop him, interrupt what he is saying and correct him. In his immediate entourage there has never been a cult of adoration or bowing and scraping, no forms of homage. But even if many of his people argue with him and are not afraid to oppose him, in the end they have usually listened to him and carried out his orders.

Arafat's senior associates, who change frequently, are also not beyond criticizing him, and it is clear that if his rule has never been easy, neither has it been easy to tolerate. In the period after the Madrid Conference (1992–1993), the heads of the Palestinian delegation, which he had appointed from the West Bank and Gaza to negotiate with Israel, rebelled against him. The delegation leader, Dr. Haidar Abdel Shafi, repeated on dozens of occasions during 1992–1993 the demand to establish a collective leadership, and he also organized a considerable support group which signed a petition in favor of this idea.

Mahmoud Abbas (Abu Mazen), the man considered second to Arafat in the PLO hierarchy after the assassination of Khalil al-Wazir (Abu Jihad) and Salah Khalaf (Abu Iyad), published announcements that the time had come to introduce new and younger blood into the top leadership. But while Abu Mazen, like many in the Palestinian leadership, criticized Arafat, he chose his words carefully. It was not that he had personal fears, but rather he feared that without Arafat the Palestinian leadership would sink into a swamp of upheavals and quarrels, leading to a chaos which would be impossible to control. Whenever Arafat's position was sapped, as in Gaza amid the struggles with Islamic fanatics at the end of 1994, Palestinian activists would be heard saying that: "It is terrible with him, but it would be catastrophic without him."

He has become famous for his unusual style of working with his own people, and in particular for his argumentativeness. Rather than persuade his listeners, he exhausts them with clichés and hollow phrases repeated over and over again. Innumerable journalistic interviews with him have turned into extended polemics rather than question-and-answer sessions. Instead of answering questions, he tends to reply with questions of his own, dragging his audience into endless arguments. Some of his staff once joked that on the rare occasions when he is alone in his office, they hear him arguing with himself in the mirror. It has been noticed that in public appearances he stammers and his for-mulations are clumsy and oversimplified. His method for empha-sizing a point is simply to repeat the same word or sentence several times. Critics call attention to the pointlessness of the interminable meetings in his office, dragged out hour after hour and ending with no clear resolutions or conclusions. "He has no sense or dimension of time," Abu Iyad once said.[9] In the end he usually makes decisions alone.

Arafat has enjoyed a mysterious sort of power, for years pre-venting anyone in the Palestinian leadership from even consider-ing his overthrow. How can this be explained? It is a power which has made him into a source of inspiration to his people. *Al-Walid,* meaning "the father" has always been one of his nicknames among the Palestinians and this title connotes the nation's found-ing father, adorned with a holy radiance.

What appears like a maze of contradictions surrounding the riddle of Arafat's leadership has for many years been a cause of common concern: to his Israeli opponents/enemies; to the politi-cal leadership and public opinion in the West; and even to many of his own people. If he is a significant figure, then it is important to understand him. Yet the mystery remains.

Nearly everyone who has researched the Middle Eastern conflict and met Arafat has puzzled over the nature of his leadership.
How is it that someone who looks so strange and is so lacking in
seriousness can at the same time be considered a statesman and
revolutionary of the first order? Politicians, researchers, commen-
tators, journalists, as well as more than a few psychologists—
all have pondered the riddle of his persona and tried to decipher
it. Most have followed the approach of one of the veterans of
Arafat's movement, Khaled al-Hassan, who once said: "But if you
understand the man Arafat, you understand the problem."[10]

One way to try to understand the man is to investigate his history. Accordingly, journalists often ask him how he came to get
involved in the Palestine problem. What caused him, as a young
man who grew up in Egypt, to become involved in political
activity in the early 1950s? When Arafat tries to answer,[11] he
seems confused and replies humorously that in the Committee of
Palestinian Students in Cairo University in 1950, they couldn't
find anyone else prepared to work twenty-four hours a day.

"Over forty years later you still don't know what made you do
it?" the reporters ask.

"Right," he says, and laughs again.

There are those who have tried to explain his lack of credibility. How, they wonder, does Arafat manage to present, sometimes
in the very same discussion, completely contradictory positions?
Is he simply lying? Why doesn't he avoid ridiculous exaggerations? Can't he distinguish between saying one thing and then
the opposite? In the past, in dozens of interviews, he has taken
the position both of seeking compromise and peace, and of bel-
ligerent intransigence. What amazes many people is that Arafat's
"thousand faces" all appear to be genuine.

The psychologist Herbert C. Kelman, who has talked to him at
length, once wrote that both "Arafat's signals of readiness for compromise and his reiterations of an uncompromising stance reflect

his true attitudes."[12] When Shimon Peres was asked his view on Arafat's lies, his answer implied that all the Arabs express themselves inexactly. "The role of the word in the Arab world is different from that in ours," Peres said. "With us, the word is a commitment and with them a word is decoration." As evidence he quoted a line from the Syrian poet Nasir Kabanni saying that the Arabs were subject for 1,500 years to "the imperialism of poetry."[13]

After his arrival in Gaza to implement the agreement he had signed with Israel, the mystery surrounding Arafat's personality began to take on new importance. Before the peace process, Arafat had been the man who personified the Palestinian problem in all its complexity. After the summer of 1994, the emphasis would pass over to the solution. At home in Gaza, can Arafat succeed as the personification of that solution?

For decades Arafat has seemed confident of possessing this ability. There was no doubt in his mind that his experience in molding the Palestinian revolution would enable him to succeed in constructing the foundations of an independent state. In a 1990 interview he said, "is there another revolution in the world which is required to market olive oil, oranges, and vegetables?"[14] And it is true that during its long years of struggle, the Palestinian revolution created a giant network of social, cultural, economic, and service institutions. At first sight, therefore, the PLO people did arrive in Gaza with the necessary experience for establishing the machinery of a state-in-the-making.

However, the problem is not only the establishment of efficient administration of a Palestinian rule, organized in the territories and led by Arafat. It is much deeper. What sort of solution does Arafat propose to the Palestinians after he did indeed represent their distress so sharply and successfully for some forty years?

Professor Edward Said, one of his former admirers, has been deeply disappointed. In his opinion Arafat has brought that Palestinian problem which he himself personified to a solution of surrender, to the "Palestinian Versailles."[15] Arafat has become in his eyes "a parody of a Latin American dictator,"[16] and there is now a danger that the Palestinian entity which will arise will be a sort of "marriage between Lebanese chaos and civil war, and the tyranny of Saddam Hussein in Iraq." At the same time the Muslim extremists and other spokespeople for the Palestinian opposition accuse Arafat of becoming an Israeli agent in Gaza. Some of these have even called publicly for Arafat's assassination (for example Ahmad Jibril, leader of the small populist Palestine Liberation Front—General Command, and Dr. Fathi Shkaki, head of the Islamic Jihad organization, both living in Damascus).

Toward what destiny has this enigmatic figure been leading the Palestinians, as well as the whole country, the whole region? Is the road leading to future progress or a dead end? The better we understand the mystery of Arafat's leadership, the better we will be able to understand and appreciate the future of the Palestinian problem and its solution.

cairo and jerusalem

A first hint to the solution of the problem of Arafat (and of the Palestinians whom he represents) lies in the question, where was he born, and who were his parents and family? This should be an easy question to answer. But as in so many subjects related to Arafat, the replies provided by him and his people on this subject are garbled and most of them contain inaccuracies, exaggerations, and even untruths. How can reaction to such a trivial question be explained? Is there some skeleton in the closet of Arafat's birth and childhood?

Anyone contacting the PLO staff in Lebanon or in Tunis, or asking the official spokespeople of the authority established in Gaza, would receive the official answer that Arafat was born in August 1929 in the Old City of Jerusalem. He himself stubbornly repeats this version[17] but he also frequently gives other answers. For example that he was born in Gaza: "I was born in Gaza, my mother died when I was four years old and I was sent to live in my uncle's house in Jerusalem."[18] The versions according to which Arafat was born in Jerusalem or in Gaza are those most often repeated, both by him and by his spokespeople. Once I even came across a claim that he was born in Acre,[19] while some speak of Nablus, Safed or Lydda, in all of which there are families bearing the Arafat name.[20]

But the truth can easily be discovered. As all his biographers note, there is ample proof that Yasser Arafat was born in Cairo. People have seen his birth certificate dated 24 August 1929[21] or examined his registration as a student at the King Fouad I University (which became Cairo University)—where the date is given as August 4th. Members of his family and their childhood neighbors and acquaintances bear witness to this, (for example, Abu Sitta's evidence).[22] There is in fact no doubt that Arafat was born in Cairo.

Arafat himself does not deny that he spent many years of his childhood in Cairo. He usually says that up to 1942, when he was thirteen, he grew up in the house where he was born in Jerusalem and only then went with his family to Egypt. How, then, can the certificates and registration of his birth in Cairo be explained? The answer given is that forgeries were carried out by his family, either because his mother acted improperly when she left his father in Cairo so as to give birth to him in Jerusalem,[23] or because the family wanted Egyptian documents so that Arafat would not face problems in being accepted by Egyptian educational institutions.

Dealing with this subject is unpalatable to Arafat and he has done his best to avoid it. For example—during his visits in Gaza at the opening of the 1994 school year, he answered pupils' questions at the Rashad al-Shawa Cultural Center in the city. One of the youngsters asked: "We know Arafat the president and the warrior, the leader and the symbol, now can you please tell us something about Arafat the child?" Arafat answered all the other questions put by the children, but passed over this one. Years before in talks with Arab journalists in Lebanon, he was asked directly: where are you from, Gaza or Jerusalem? He replied: "My father was from Gaza and my mother from Jerusalem, from the Abu-Saud family."[24]

This quibbling answer is indeed correct. His father, whose full name was Abdel Raouf Arafat al-Qudwa al-Husseini, was born in

Gaza, while the origin of his family was in neighboring Khan Yunis. He married Zahwa Abu Saud from Jerusalem. The couple lived in Gaza and Jerusalem for some time and in 1927 went to Egypt, where they lived in the middle-class Al Sakakini neighborhood. It was here that Yasser Arafat was born two years later. He was the sixth child and he has a younger brother. When he was four, his mother died in Cairo from a kidney illness and he and his young brother were sent for some time to the mother's family in Jerusalem. It is difficult to know exactly how long they stayed with the Abu Saud family in Jerusalem or if they stayed for some time in Gaza with their father's al-Qudwa family. In any case, their irregular stays with the families in Palestine were short and Arafat spent most of his childhood and school years in his father's house in Cairo.

His father remarried twice after his first wife's death, and the eldest daughter of the family, Inam, had most of the responsibility for bringing up Yasser Arafat.

A number of versions have been given concerning the reasons for Arafat's parents' emigration from Palestine to Egypt. While his father was a small merchant from the lower middle class, his mother came from a relatively respected Jerusalem family. Apparently his father's business did not succeed. The father's mother (Arafat's grandmother) was of Egyptian origin (from the Radwan family) and some of the family claimed that she had inheritance rights over a large land asset in Cairo, called Hadikat al-Izbakia. Arafat has mentioned this asset on several occasions, saying it was now the property of the Egyptian Ein Shamas University.

In any case, the father devoted his 25 years in Egypt to a hopeless legal struggle to win this inheritance. This became an obsession and he spent years filing papers and waiting for the courts, while continuing to make a living as a small businessman. The Egyptian legal system considered him a nuisance, repeatedly rejected his claims and caused him great disappointment and bitterness. In 1952, with the Free Officers' coup abolishing the monarchy, the law in Egypt was changed to restrict rights of inheritance and all hope of winning the property was lost. Arafat's father returned to the Gaza Strip and soon died there. He was buried in the small cemetery in the center of the town of Khan Yunis. Yasser Arafat did not attend the funeral.

Fifty years later, in May 1994, Arafat entered the district of Palestinian self-rule for the first time, traveling by car in an official ceremonial convoy from the border at Rafah. I was among a few people waiting in the Khan Yunis market in case he should stop on the way and visit his father's grave. He did not do so and it is doubtful if he has ever visited the small graveyard. Arafat's family connections were never especially strong, probably because he grew up far away from his extended family in Palestine. His brothers and sisters remained in Cairo, and established their families there.

Yasser Arafat himself left Cairo in 1957, after completing his engineering studies at the University, and went to work as an engineer in Kuwait. Since then he has never returned to live in Egypt and in the course of his life he has wandered unceasingly through all the Arab states along the path taken by the Palestinian national movement.

What, then, is wrong with this biography? What is missing in it? Yasser Arafat was not indeed born in Palestine and there may perhaps be some surprise that "Mr. Palestine" was not born in the country which he purports to symbolize. But nobody contests his Palestinian origins. For hundreds of years, until after the First World War, the whole of the Arab world and especially the region known as the Fertile Crescent constituted one political unity. For four centuries it was ruled by the Ottoman Empire. From time to time, Arab groups and families passed from place to place: from Damascus to Jerusalem, from Hebron to Cairo. Members of the elite families of Jaffa, Haifa, Gaza and Nazareth married into elite families from Syria and Lebanon. Villagers and Bedouin passed undisturbed through the various regions. Rich people from the Levant owned land in Palestine and those from Nablus had assets in eastern Jordan. Most were and remained of the same religion, spoke the same language, Arabic, and were faithful to the same culture and Islamic tradition.

So why should it trouble Yasser Arafat if his family emigrated in the 1920s from Palestine to Egypt, and if he was Egyptian-born? Why should he feel a need to misrepresent and distort his biography? Could anyone doubt that he is a Palestinian? In any case, from the beginnings of modern nationalism many examples can be found of national leaders who were born outside their homelands. Napoleon was born in Corsica, and Hitler in Austria. National feelings often well up especially powerfully among people living outside their homelands.

In the case of Yasser Arafat, the distortions, evasions and blurring over of the facts came in the wake of a contradiction between his personal experience as a child in Egypt, and what one may call the "Palestine experience" which he wanted to represent. "To be a Palestinian is a question of political outlook rather than of geographical origins," Eastern Studies Professor Bernard Lewis once remarked. Arafat never had any doubts concerning his political outlook, but his Egyptian background could only damage his image.

For example, over the many years in which Arafat has led the Palestinians he has never succeeded in overcoming the dissatisfaction felt by many people at his speaking with a strong Egyptian accent. Nizar Amar, who first met him early in 1968 in Jordan, before the Palestinians knew from radio and TV appearances how Arafat spoke, tells how he was amazed by his strong Egyptian accent.[25] He had heard in secret of the revered Palestinian commander—and now suddenly it transpires that he speaks not with a Palestinian, but with an Egyptian accent! What is the meaning of this? Salah Khalaf (Abu Iyad), Arafat's close friend throughout their common political careers, also recounts that at their first meeting in Cairo he was offended by such a heavy Egyptian accent in someone who aspired to be the Chairperson of the Palestinian students.

The special accents, the intonations, of various regions of Palestine are an important element in the national consciousness of the Palestinian Arabs. There is a difference between the accents of town-dwellers, Bedouin, villagers, and between people from different regions, as well as social classes. My own teacher of spoken Arabic at Jerusalem University, Professor Moshe Piantana, could discern after hearing only a few words of Arabic from what part of the country the speaker came. So every Palestinian who heard Arafat speak knew that he was not from Palestine but from Egypt.

Over the many years which he spent in Kuwait and in Lebanon, Arafat succeeded to some extent in losing his Egyptian accent. However, when he is heard shouting in anger, speaking hurriedly, enthusiastically, or excitedly, the Egyptian accent once again takes over. Almost certainly Arafat has at times felt uneasy about this accent which sounds foreign in the ears of his people.

Today the accent with which one speaks has become very important politically, one of the central elements of the Palestinian identity. This was not necessarily so before 1948. For example, Sheikh Izz al-Din al-Qassam, who was the first hero of Palestinian martyrology, was born in Syria and came as a young preacher to a Haifa mosque in 1925. In the early 1930s, the Syrian sheikh organized armed attacks against the Jews, and in 1935 he was killed in a battle with the British army.

Sheikh al-Qassam is considered in the Arab world to be the harbinger of the Palestinian revolt against the British which erupted in 1936. Decades later, with the outbreak of the Intifada against Israeli rule in the West Bank and Gaza, terrorist groups among the Muslim extremists (the Hamas movement) adopted his name. Perhaps it is not by chance that Yasser Arafat too has often recalled the martyred Sheikh al-Qassam as one of his heroes: they share a community of fate as Palestinian heroes who were not born in Palestine.

In the course of the struggle against the Jewish population and Zionism, to be born in a house in a Palestinian village, or in one of the small neighborhoods of the Palestinian towns, became a central component of the Palestinian claim for ownership of the country. This was understandable. The Palestinians used the fact of their being natives of the country as their most important political and moral argument against the Jewish immigrants. The Jews were foreign invaders who had come to plunder the houses and land of the people of the country. After 1948, emphasis upon the nativity of Palestinian Arabs was considerably strengthened when half of them (numbering about 750,000) lost their homes, their land and their property, and became impoverished refugees in camps in the Gaza Strip, in the West Bank and in Syria and Lebanon. They demanded to return to the places where they had been born and where their forefathers had lived for hundreds of years.

Their connection with the land, the village and childhood landscapes, became for the Palestinians the focus of their identity. Most of the Palestinian population was overwhelmed by their sense of loss and by having been forcibly uprooted in 1948. The poet Mahmoud Darwish saw his people as "expelled from history and from homeland."[26] They became "victims of the map"[27] or "people of nowhere" in the words of the Palestinian-American Edward Said.[28]

How was Arafat, who was indeed of Palestinian origin but born in Cairo, to react to this? He personally had no memories of a lost childhood home. Nor had he undergone the trauma of a refugee torn up from his roots. He had possessed no "place" from which he had been driven out. His family lived outside the borders of that map where the Palestinians were the victims.

His father and mother had not left Palestine because of the "Zionist invasion" or because of British intrigues or Imperialist plots. Abdel Raouf Arafat al-Qudwa left Palestine only in a dubious pursuit of wealth, the uncertain inheritance of an Egyptian mother. The emigration of Arafat's parents constituted a sort of abandonment of the homeland, or desertion from the struggle. From the point of view of many Palestinians, this could have undermined the Palestinian claim to a deep connection with their homeland.

But Yasser Arafat was not unaffected by the new reality which had been created in Palestine in 1948. During the war he served for a short time in Gaza as a volunteer soldier and saw the streams of refugees there. Several of the sons of the refugees were among his student friends who had studied with him at Cairo University just after the war. They spoke, wrote and sang of the terrible tragedy, of the Palestinian holocaust; *The Jerusalem Holocaust and Paradise Lost* was the title of a well-known book by the Palestinian historian Araf el-Araf who documented the destruction of the homeland. The significance of the homeland for the first generation of refugees was quite direct and concrete: the field, the plot of land, the olive tree, the verandah, the well in the courtyard—all things which had been lost. The personal identity of the refugees was connected with very particular places: with the sand dunes of Ashdod, the orange groves of Ramle, the Jaffa port. The burden of yearning was well-defined and was vividly expressed in refugee literature: the loss was an abomination, a disgrace, an affront and a humiliation. Arafat certainly felt a community of fate with the suffering of his people but was obviously conscious of the fact that he and his family had not themselves taken part in this painful experience.

Years later, many of the first Palestinian national activists and Arafat's contemporaries at school wrote of the bitter memories which had molded their political world. Salah Khalaf (Abu Iyad) described his childhood in Jaffa and the terrible day when they had gathered together to flee by sea, carrying their load of suitcases and bundles. In the crowded boat a woman found that one of her children had disappeared and she burst into shrieks of anguish, jumping into the sea in her desperation. Her husband, who was unable to stop her, jumped in after her and both of them were lost in the waves. The young Salah Kalaf was in that boat and like all the passengers suffered from shock. He arrived in Cairo in 1951 and was for many years Arafat's closest friend and partner in the leadership (until his murder in 1991 in Tunis by one of his bodyguards who belonged to Abu Nidal's people).

Another Palestinian leader, George Habash, wrote a personal account of the battles in Lydda, of the Arab defeat and expulsion from the town of his birth. Khalil al-Wazir (Abu Jihad), Arafat's friend and deputy, born in Ramle (and murdered in Tunis in 1988 during an Israeli raid) recorded the horrors he experienced as a child with his family during the expulsion from the town of Ramle. Hundreds of others who witnessed the disaster described it from the viewpoint of their own personal anguish over the loss of their homeland, "The land of sad oranges," as Palestinian writer Ghassan Kanafani called it, which they loved so dearly.

Those who grew up as the children of refugees, like the attorney Raja Shehadeh, also claim that their love for the land of their country is the result of very personal and intimate experiences, steeped in "erotic feelings." Shehadeh walks on the soil of the hills near Ramallah, unconsciously enjoys the touch of the hard earth under the soles of his feet, smells the thyme, looks for a long time at the olive trees. Desire for the earth which the Jews threaten to take over arouses such physical jealousy within him that he calls himself the country's pornographer. The smell of the village land, hugging the fig and fruit trees, uncompromising attachment to the earth—all these are very personal expressions with which the Palestinian ethos has been replete since the 1950s.

The only one of the eminent people in the Palestinian leadership who has never written memoirs or descriptions of this sort is Yasser Arafat. There is no record of his personal perceptions of such experiences. In fact he himself lost nothing. If in the words of one Palestinian literary critic[29] "in this world a person lives in a certain place, but for the Palestinian, the place lives within the person," Arafat simply lacked these basic personal experiences which the people of his Palestinian generation went through. He had no childhood home in the lost homeland, no plot of land which became the possession of someone else, no close relatives who were transformed into destitute refugees.

However, Arafat was familiar with the term Exile. Perhaps he understood it even better than other Palestinians. It can be noted paradoxically that Yasser Arafat lived the Palestinian Exile before such a thing actually existed. For he grew up in Egypt as the son of a family which was alien, not of the place. He had no close relatives near him, who in the traditional Arab family provide social and economic support. After his mother's death, even his own small family disintegrated. In his Cairo neighborhood he was surely known as a foreigner. The neighborhood children must have pointed to him as a kid who didn't belong, a stranger who came from elsewhere. He was made aware of his Palestinian identity in Egypt, in a way that youngsters of his age who grew up in Palestine were not.

Fawaz Turki, who was born and until 1948 lived in the little town of Balad al-Sheikh on the northern edge of Haifa, describes this sort of Palestinian experience. Arriving with his family in Lebanon as refugees, he noted that "the great expanses of the Arab world are not great enough to absorb those banished from their country."[30] "Go back to where you came from," cried the Lebanese kids in a Beirut neighborhood, "you're only sons-of-bitches who sold your land to the Jews." Fawaz Turki says in amazement that until then he had not been at all conscious of being a Palestinian.[31] His Palestinian identity became clear to him only on arriving as a refugee in Lebanon. In the village where he was born, as everywhere in the Arab population of the country, people didn't bother to remind each other of what was self-evident: that they were all sons of the Palestinian homeland.

When Arafat started his political life among the Palestinian students at Cairo University, he set out along a winding trail of desperate attempts to overcome the contradiction between his personal biography and the collective Palestinian biography. The distortions and cover-ups about his place of birth have been carried out against this background. On the one hand he had a deep Palestinian political consciousness, and on the other, he lacked that elementary personal experience of painfully losing a plundered childhood landscape.

When people worried him with questions about his parents and childhood, Arafat was ready to speak only about his mother's family home in Jerusalem, where, as we have said, he spent some time as a small child after his mother's death. The reason is clear: the house of this family, Abu Saud, was extremely appropriate for a Palestinian leader to grow up in. It was very close to the wall of the Temple Mount, and a few yards away from the Dome of the Rock Mosque, the holy symbol of Arab and Muslim Jerusalem. Just beyond the courtyard of the Abu Saud home was the Western Wall, known as the "Wailing Wall," which has served ever since the early Jewish settlement in Palestine as a bone of contention and resentment between Jews and Muslims.

Immediately after the 1967 war, the Israeli government widened the Western Wall square and for this purpose tore down the houses in the adjacent Arab neighborhood. The ancient house of the Abu Saud family was among those demolished. Since it was a large house which stood out above all the others at the entrance to the Temple Mount, its destruction aroused wide public response and media attention.

Yasser Arafat, who in 1967 was not a well-known public figure, spent several weeks during the autumn of that year in the
West Bank, but it is doubtful if he witnessed the demolition
of the house. Nevertheless, on the few occasions when he has
spoken of his childhood, he generally mentioned the Abu Saud
house and its destruction along with vague hints and fragmentary
remarks on childhood memories from Jerusalem: how he saw
fighting in the streets and the arrest of members of his family.
These remarks serve to link him with the Palestine experience of
a childhood home, one situated in the very heart of the homeland, which was a focus for the struggle with the Jews, and was
eventually destroyed by the Israelis.

As far as one can ascertain, Arafat did live in this house as a
child for about three years, from 1933 to 1936, from the age of
four to seven. Perhaps he visited it on a few occasions afterward.
Vague memories from this period have helped him to fill in the
gap between his personal experience and his Palestinian national
sentiments. Even in his first interviews as PLO leader, in 1969,
his language mixed the singular and plural: "I am a refugee, we
are a people of refugees, do you know the significance of being
a refugee? I am a person who lacks everything, I have nothing,
because I was driven into exile and my homeland was taken
from me."[32]

This is not exactly a lie. There were many other Palestinians
who did not suffer personally in the 1948 war, who stayed in their
houses in the country, but saw themselves as victims uprooted
from their homeland because they lost their sovereignty over
Palestine. In some cases when interviewers have pressed Arafat
and demanded to know exactly where he was born, he has
replied simply: "I was not born until I became Abu Ammar." This
is perhaps the most authentic of his answers. Abu Ammar was to
become his most accepted revolutionary name and Arafat has
unquestionably invested his whole identity in the struggle for the

Palestinian revolution. His personal past, and the place where he was born and brought up, are irrelevant. The Palestinian revolution which he represents, with its longing for a homeland, has become for him the truest expression of his birth.

what's in a name?

Analogous to the complications concerning Yasser Arafat's birthplace are those surrounding the very name and identity of the
man. During the civil war in Lebanon, when the PLO Chairman
had already been a recognized figure for some fifteen years, Arab
journalists who interviewed him in Beirut about his identity
were still mystified. They conducted this familiar slogan-ridden
exchange:

Who exactly are you?—I am a fighter in the ranks of the Palestinian revolution.—Is your name Yasser Arafat?—That is the name
by which I have been known since my university days.—Where
are you from?—From the very heart of the Palestinian people.—
The Palestinians would like to know more about their leader;
permit us to ask once again who you are?—I am a son of the
Palestinian people and a fighter in the ranks of the revolution.[33]

Arafat could not be drawn into answering more exactly even
on the simple question of his real name. But this had become
known in one of the first publications about him, written in 1970
by the Israeli journalist Ehud Ya'ari. It is Abdel Rahman Abdel
Raouf Arafat al-Qudwa al-Husseini[34] (the long name includes
the first name, that of the father, and the names of the extended
family). In most later publications, his first name appears as
Mohammed (instead of or along with Abdel Rahman), perhaps

because of the fact that in Egypt it is customary to add the name of the Prophet Mohammed to one's private names. If Arafat had been an ordinary person, perhaps he would have been called Mohammed Arafat, or Abdel Rahman al-Qudwa. But from a young age changes were already occurring in his name. His friends at high school in Cairo added the name Yasser, which means easygoing. Ever since then he has been known among his acquaintances as Yasser Arafat.

From his first steps in founding the Fatah movement in the late 1950s, Arafat used his real name very little, adopting a number of secret names. At first, this seems understandable considering his underground activities which made him a constant fugitive. But while all his colleagues had one underground name, generally that of their oldest son, Arafat changed names all the time.

There were periods when he was called "the Doctor" or "Dr. Mohammed" or "Dr. Fawzi Arafat" or "Abu Mohammed," "Dr. Husseini" or "Raouf" (after his father). But the nickname best loved by him and by the Palestinians was "Abu Ammar." Arafat likes it because one of the Prophet Mohammed's friends and the commander of his army was called Ammar Abu Yasser. There is a tradition in Islam that this ancient hero suffered agony for his faith. Since the custom in Palestinian society is that on reaching maturity, an unmarried man is called after his father, Arafat chose as his patronymic a name hinting at the Islamic hero. As it turned out, the name Abu Ammar has won great prestige among his people: they use this name and only this name.

Arafat almost never mentions the original names of his family. Some have claimed that he was particularly anxious to shed the name al-Husseini because he did not want to be identified with the Mufti Haj Amin al-Husseini, the Palestinian leader in the Mandatory period, and with that leadership which brought about the disastrous defeat in 1948. "If there is anything I don't want to be, it is Haj Amin al-Husseini," Arafat has often said to acquaintances, like Edward Said.[35] However, there is no actual connection between the Gaza Husseinis, to whom Arafat is related, and the aristocratic Husseini family of Jerusalem.

Arafat is fond of some of the other nicknames given to him as marks of appreciation, such as *al-Hatiar*, "the old man," and *al-Walid,* "the father." The significance of both these names is that they attribute to Arafat the characteristic of father of the nation, which certainly flatters him.

As with his birthplace, Arafat prefers names that give him a collective and not a private identity. Arafat changed his place of birth from Cairo to Jerusalem since it was unthinkable that the "Palestinian problem" could have been born in Cairo. In the same way, when his personal names became burdensome he discarded them. He sees his real names as those of the nation and the revolution which he leads. It is even possible to understand this as an attempt to wipe out his private identity, or at least to make it irrelevant. For him, what is important is only his public-political identity as personifying the Palestinian problem.

I saw this in Arafat's public appearances when he arrived in Gaza to live among his people in the summer of 1994. Everywhere I accompanied him as a journalist, he was received by the masses with the traditional rhythmic cry "In our spirit and our blood we will redeem you, Abu Ammar" (that is, we will sacrifice in spirit and blood for you, Abu Ammar). Arafat always tried to silence the applauders and demanded they change the cry to say they would sacrifice for Palestine, instead of for Abu Ammar. This happened time and time again. In one place, the big refugee camp of Jabalya, I heard one of the Chairman's assistants say that Arafat would prefer they call out no names or nicknames, for his real name and family name is—Palestine.

This effort to blot out his identity as a private person is an important key to understanding not only Arafat's personality but, more importantly—his political role. Those nearest to him have understood his efforts. Abu Jihad, who for years was closest to him, formulated this in words which are not merely flattery: "The secret of Arafat is that he lives all of our emotions. Arafat is not just a political symbol. We sense and we know that he is living all of our fears, all of our dreams and all of our suffering. When any Palestinian is suffering, Arafat feels the pain. When one of our fighters is killed, a small part of Arafat is killed . . . In this one person is all of us, all of our emotions, all of our strength, all of our weaknesses, all of our contradictions."[36]

Arafat and his colleagues did everything possible to ensure that this identification of the man with the nation would be accepted by the broad public. For a long period all his partners in the Fatah leadership worked on this political goal. So when journalists in Lebanon once determined that "Arafat is both the problem and the solution," this could have been viewed as an exaggerated attempt to personify the Palestine problem. But years later, it would turn out that the effort had succeeded not only among Arafat's sympathizers but also among his enemies.

When the government of Israel under Yitzhak Rabin decided to recognize the PLO and to enter into direct negotiations with Arafat, many concerned Israelis asked, how can we erase the memories of the past which are associated with him? In a series of public appearances, Yitzhak Rabin answered that in practice there is no alternative. Israel must talk to Arafat because with the Palestinians everything comes back to him, and he is the only one who can decide. Thus Israel too recognized what all the other states in the world had gradually come to understand: that Arafat, although not possessing the power and authority of a head of state, has indeed succeeded in obscuring his private personality so as rightfully to become both the spokesman of his people and the symbol personifying their distress and aspirations. He has become *homo Palestinus*.

Arafat has achieved this through his outward appearance too. For years he has tried to ensure that his looks would be as far as possible symbolic of the Palestinian collective. At his own initiative, he cultivated an appearance whose various components each held political and national significance. Of these, the first component and the most conspicuous was his unshaven face.

It is hard to describe the extent to which "the hairs on his face" in the words of Israeli Prime Minister Menachem Begin, have been the object of public opinion all over the world. Anyone collecting the press cuttings dealing with Arafat's unshaven beard could fill volumes. Journalists preparing to interview Arafat would compile a long list of questions on politics, terrorism, and the future of the Palestinians. However, they soon discovered that what interested the public no less (and perhaps more) was his unshaven face. "Mr. Chairman, why don't you at least shave?" asked journalist J. D. Allman[37] in an interview for *Vanity Fair,* adding "When people in America heard I was going to meet you, every one of them asked the same question. It wasn't about terrorism or Israel; they ask, why don't you shave?"

Going over the newspaper reports which have appeared on Yasser Arafat over the years, I have found innumerable references to the subject of his shaving. In all of them, those who met him examined his face carefully. Some thought that his unshaven face was repulsive, reflected evil, created a dirty impression; others conjectured a skin disease. Some observed that it was a sparse beard whose grey streaks created in television pictures a false impression of dirt.[38]

Books about him have also gone into the subject. Rashida Mahran,[39] writing on Arafat's "shaving history" reveals that he once shaved when leaving Beirut for a meeting with Sadat, before Sadat's visit to Jerusalem caused a rupture in their relations. But the reason for his shaving was not to feel comfortable or to look good. Arafat has never spoken of himself in those terms. No, he says, he shaved in order to fool would-be assassins![40] The beard in this instance is therefore explained as part of a costume, worn to serve the political needs of the Palestinian people.

On many other occasions, he has answered questions about not shaving with a surprising political-ideological message. Instead of a personal reply to a question about personal habits, he has given what might be called a public, collective answer of the Palestinians. His favorite answer has been that shaving would take several minutes of his time and as the representative of the Palestinians he has no time for this. On several occasions he has even calculated how long shaving takes and multiplied it by days and months, concluding that, altogether, a man could waste half a year or more of his life on shaving. Arafat says he doesn't want to waste this time and prefers to devote it to the Palestinian people.[41] Another response is that he spends part of his time with Palestinian fighters on the battlefield, where there are no facilities for people to pamper themselves with shaving.

So we see how a minor personal question can become for him a symbolic expression of national values. The Palestinians are a poor people, migrants, constantly struggling, without the time needed for attentions to personal appearances, like shaving. Just how fascinating this subject is to the public can be seen from an article by the American journalist Mary Anne Weaver who stayed in Arafat's house in Tunis.[42] She tells how she went into his personal shower and discovered that he owns both a razor and a pair of trimming shears. That she felt it important to tell her readers of her visit to Arafat's bathroom is interesting in itself.

In his younger days Arafat was preoccupied by the great public reaction aroused by his unprepossessing appearance. He received reports on the subject almost every day, telling him how ugly he was, how fleshy his lips, that he was short and inclined to be fat. But most of the attention was directed to his perennial army uniform, to his revolver, and to the kaffiyeh on his bald head. Like the sidearm, the uniform symbolized his national orientation, the "armed struggle" in whose name he founded the reborn Palestinian movement. A standard army uniform tends to erase individual identity and stress belonging to a collective, and Arafat never takes off his uniform. In fact, he has apparently never owned any clothes other than a few sets of uniforms, adorned with several small, colored metal badges and with colored pens, his great love. In reports on his few hours of sleep (for instance while flying) and odd moments devoted to physical exercise every day, we are informed that he changes his uniform for sweatsuits, which are also standard, impersonal clothes. To this day he has resisted giving up his style of dress, his uniform, and his sidearm. His assistants urged him repeatedly to wear civilian clothes to the signing ceremony of the peace agreement with Israel. He appeared dressed as always.

Is there any importance to all this? Apparently, there is. What looks at first like a media gimmick has helped Arafat get through to the popular consciousness the world over. Liberal circles in the West in the 1970s and '80s were attracted by the romanticism of a figure who looked ridiculous but who spoke passionately of a struggle for freedom and national liberation. He excited the imagination, aroused curiosity, not only because of the cause he proclaimed but also because of his special appearance.

His people, the Palestinians, also showed great interest in his dress. They liked his kaffiyeh. Arafat began wearing it when he first traveled to Europe in 1956 as a member of the Palestinian Students' delegation from Egypt. The people at the Prague conference were impressed by the large white scarf which Arafat suddenly pulled out—of course with the idea of drawing general attention. This is the traditional headdress in the countryside in some parts of the Arab world, and in the late 1930s, when groups of country people from among the Palestinian Arabs led the revolt against the British rule and the Jewish community (the "Great Revolt"), they demanded that the urban sections of the Arab population get rid of the Turkish "Tarbush" hat, as well as European hats, and wear the kaffiyeh instead.[43] Anyone not doing so was attacked and beaten.

Later on the kaffiyeh took on a more particular political significance. The children of the Intifada in Gaza and the West Bank
covered their heads with the kaffiyeh during demonstrations and
marches, and when they threw stones at Israeli soldiers. Saeb
Erakat, who was a member of the Palestinian delegation to the
Madrid talks, wound it around his neck at the cermonial session of
the conference, thereby arousing great anger among the Israelis. In
the subsequent discussions in Washington among the various delegations, Dr. Haidar Abdel Shafi, chairman of the Palestinian delegation, who wore a European hat, was criticized by the Palestinian
public, which demanded that he remove the foreign headgear.

Arafat has added to his wearing of the kaffiyeh a special way of
tying it so that it has a sharp end. When asked for the meaning
of this, he replies that in this way the kaffiyeh creates the outline
of the map of Palestine. He wears it constantly, except when he
dons an army fatigue cap.

None of the elements of Arafat's "look" were created by public
relations or publicity experts. They are stamped by his own character and personality and they make his appearance theatrical and
provocative in a calculated way. In the words of one of his staff:
"Arafat is extremely careful about his careless appearance."[44]

Everything serves the political purpose, the aim of fostering
the personal-collective challenge of the Palestinian entity which
Arafat has cultivated. The lies and sophistry around his personal
details, his many names, his acting, the gray-streaked beard, his
style of dress, the carrying of arms—for the media all these are
merely a game, but they were adopted by Arafat as an integral
part of his political stand. When he is photographed in the company of world leaders, unshaven and wearing rumpled fatigues, all
the rest smart and polished in their fine suits—he stands out
immediately, attracting attention, arousing surprise and curiosity.
This symbolic representation of the Palestinian people is part of
the persistent pattern, a clue to the enigma, and has become a
curious and clever celebrity image in its own right.

from arabs to palestinians

No less than his personality, Yasser Arafat's political path appears tortuous, wayward, replete with contradictions and question marks. His political enemies and friends alike have turned time and again into critics. Friends have become enemies and enemies friends. After the Camp David accords of 1978, Anwar Sadat's Egypt was for Arafat the most despicable of all the Arab states. "Sadat sold Palestine for a handful of Sinai sand; even King Farouk would not have dared to do this," he said.[45] Yet within two or three years, though it had made no change in policy, Egypt became a most loyal ally. Arafat has had similar relations with all the Arab states, from King Hassan's Morocco in the west to Saddam Hussein's Iraq in the east. All are brothers, all are traitors.

Since he was first jailed in Gamal Abdel Nasser's Egypt in 1954, he has been in turn imprisoned and expelled, fought and made up, in a series of Arab states. At least twice he has made agreements with King Hussein on cooperation and confederation, but he also accused the king of destroying the Palestinian people when he fought against the PLO in the Jordanian civil war of 1970–1971. "Hussein killed and wounded 25,000 of our people," Arafat has said more than once.[46] At the Arab summit conference in Morocco in 1974, an attempt by Palestinians to murder the Jordanian king was organized, either on Arafat's initiative or with his knowledge (though he denied this). The attempt failed when Moroccan security forces discovered the plotters.[47]

The Ba'ath regime in Syria was for years (1960–1966) the most faithful ally of Arafat and his people. He called Syria his "second homeland,"[48] but after a time, the Syrian regime became a bitter opponent. In 1966 Arafat sat in prison in Damascus and the Syrians persecuted him relentlessly. Years later, when he was more powerful, the Syrians organized a rebellion against him in Lebanon, fought him and killed many of his people (1983).

In Lebanon Arafat also spent time in jail (1965). Beirut was his residence from 1970 to 1982, while he ceaselessly maneuvered between the different Lebanese factions, making alliances with them and fighting against them all in turn. He always took care to declare that he was not interfering in Lebanon's internal affairs. However, when asked in later years whether he would be capable of establishing proper government in the West Bank and Gaza Strip, he answered: "How can one ask such a question? After all, I ruled over Lebanon for twelve years."[49]

The history of his ideological positions over the years toward the Arab states looks like that of a man for all seasons. He is an orthodox Muslim and conservative statesman to the Saudis. To the revolutionary regimes he presents himself as a knight of the secular and democratic state. He has also been considered a fanatic Muslim and it was on the basis of his connections with the Muslim Brotherhood that he was first arrested in 1954 in Egypt. Yet, he is also a socialist and a prominent member of the Socialist International. No less close than his connection with fundamentalist Islamic regimes from Iran to Sudan are his strong ties with communist regimes of the former USSR, China, Cuba, Vietnam, and the former Czechoslovakia, with whom he has showed an ideological affinity, "a partnership of revolutionaries." Considering these transformations, his every political step appears at first sight so cynical that one may ask—why should he be believed?

The Saudi Arabian poet Ghassan al-Immam once described Arafat as follows:

> *This old man is a sportsman without a playground,*
> *But he plays with all the balls and on all the grounds,*
> *The problem is that in soccer he handles the ball*
> *In basketball he uses his feet*
> *And in handball his head.*
> *When the referee catches him he insists that someone else take the rap,*
> *He is never thrown out because he has no replacement*
> *No replacement could foul like he does,*
> *And when he loses the game, he wins the applause of the masses.*[50]

The list of Arafat's denunciations of Israel is almost endless. Shortly after his speech at the UN proffering both an olive branch and a gun, he declared in Beirut that his people were stuggling against "the new embodiment of Nazi Fascism, represented by Israel's military force."[51] In a previous and well-known interview with Oriana Fallaci in the spring of 1970 he had said: "We shall never stop until we can go back home and Israel is destroyed . . . revolutionary violence is the only means for the liberation of the land of our forefathers . . . the elimination of Zionism from Palestine in all its political, economic and military aspects . . . peace for us means Israel's destruction and nothing else."[52]

In another place he said: "We will take apart the machinery of the state of Israel . . . and send the invaders to Europe or to their other lands of origin."[53] Even in later years he contemptously rejected all ideas of autonomy as an intermediary stage (which had been agreed upon with Sadat at Camp David) and also had reservations over any Palestinian connection with Jordan. A writer for the Egyptian opposition paper *Al-Sha'ab* asked Arafat why he would not agree to autonomy as an intermediary stage:

Arafat: "In 1948 we Palestinians were told to wait: we waited 17 years and established the Palestinian revolution. Another 33 years have passed—will we now establish autonomy under Israeli sponsorship? And afterwards autonomy under United Nations sponsorship?"

Question: "What about a Palestinian state which would be connected with Jordan?"

Arafat: "The idea is rejected."

Question: "And what about a Palestinian state connected with Israel?"

Arafat: "The idea is rejected." (17 January 1981)

His description of Israel, which had become routine in former years, spoke of the Zionist State as the watchdog of imperialism. In his words, it was established as "a racist entity in the region, following the first discoveries of oil in the Gulf . . ." and it had "begun its aggression at the Basle conference in 1897 at the initiative of the Rothschild, Simon and Lazare families."[54] As usual with Arafat, these attacks were accompanied by dubious historical observations.

This is the background to the general question of how seriously Israel should regard agreements with him and his aspirations for "a peace of the brave" which he has expressed time and again since 1988. Yet in spite of all Arafat's political and ideological acrobatics, there runs through his convoluted political career one straight connecting line. His anger toward the Arab brothers and his lack of confidence in them shaped his political course and was to a degree the reason for the change years later in his attitude to Israel.

One can sum up Arafat's guiding principle with a sentence he himself frequently repeats: "The truth is that the Arab regimes betrayed me," he answered when one of his biographers asked him what conclusion he reached from what he learned and experienced on the battlefield in Palestine.[55] He has referred in the same vein to Arab treason whenever asked of his conclusions from his experience in Palestine in 1948, and from the major political

twists and turns he has made with the Palestinian movement start-
ing in Cairo during the 1940s and '50s, and continuing in Jordan,
Syria, Lebanon, Tunis, and even with the agreement with Israel for
the establishment of Palestinian rule in "Gaza and Jericho first."

"What treason?" one may ask. Didn't the Arab states struggle
and fight for the Palestinian cause for decades? As a youth and
young man, Arafat saw the situation differently. As we have seen,
he developed a clear Palestinian identity and consciousness from
growing up as an alien immigrant in Cairo. He came to know the
problems of his people in the small Palestinian community which
congregated in Cairo after the Second World War. Arafat was 16
or 17 years old when the Mufti of Jerusalem Haj Amin al-Husseini arrived in Cairo and assembled his supporters and sympathizers. The Mufti, having been expelled from Palestine by the
British, had spent the war years in Nazi Germany, where he tried
to muster Arab and Muslim support for the Axis powers as part of
their struggle against British rule in Palestine. After the German
defeat he was taken prisoner by the French and detained as part-
prisoner part-guest. With the danger of being tried for war crimes
hanging over his head, he went in June 1946 to Egypt, where he
started preparations for intensifying the struggle in Palestine.

At least two of the heterogeneous personalities who came to
Haj al-Husseini's Cairo court were important for Arafat. The first
was Sheikh Hassan Abu Saud from Jerusalem, a relative of Arafat
from his mother's side. The Sheikh was a prominent personality
among the Palestinian Arabs, an orthodox follower of the Mufti
from the religious establishment in Jerusalem. The British had
arrested him during the war, exiling him to Seychelles, from
where he was freed in 1945 and came to Cairo.

The second was Abdel Kader al-Husseini, a Palestinian personality esteemed because he was among the few from the aristocratic Arab families who had joined the fighters in the battlefield
and commanded guerilla groups in the Palestinian revolt of the

late 1930s. Abdel Kader was in Iraq during the war years (assisting the anti-British revolt) and later in Saudi Arabia. He came to Cairo with his family, including his small son, born in 1941—Faisal al-Husseini, later a prominent leader, and a follower of Arafat in east Jerusalem. The young al-Husseini would remember later, "we read verses from the Koran together."[56]

One cannot measure just how much these two personalities influenced the young Arafat. Like most of the Palestinian community in Cairo, he visited the Mufti's court, talked to his relative Sheikh Abu Saud and made contact with Abdel Kader el-Husseini who was then engaged in organizing Arab fighters in Palestine. Even before then, Abdel Kadar had studied in Cairo, where he set up the first organization of Palestinian students. It appears that Arafat, along with other boys, set out under Abdel Kadar's command several times for villages and Bedouin tribes where they bought arms and ammunition to be smuggled into Palestine. His sister Inam recalled later, "as a youngster, he very much liked soldiers' games."

In the summer of 1947 Arafat completed high school and registered for studies in engineering at King Fouad I University in Cairo. At the end of that year a war broke out in Palestine between Arab and Jewish units following the United Nations resolution of 29 November to partition Palestine into two states. In the winter of 1948 the fighting intensified. The British announced that they would soon leave the country and in the spring came the first victories of the Jewish forces. The first wave of Arab refugees also rolled into exile.

A pan-Arab initiative sent groups of volunteer fighters to Palestine from throughout the Arab world. Among them was the "Rescue Army" commanded by the Syrian officer Fawzi al-Qaukji and volunteer units from the Muslim Brothers in Egypt. In spite of the distress in his homeland, Arafat stayed in Egypt and continued his university studies.

Arafat's inaction should be seen against the background of a general belief or even certainty among Palestinians that the Arab world could solve their problems with relative ease. Under British inspiration, the Arab League had been established at the end of the the Second World War. This was the first shaky framework constructed to support the dream of creating Arab unity. The Palestinian leadership had disintegrated following the failure of its revolt in the late 1930s. Hundreds had fled or had been exiled from the country. Alone, the Palestinians lacked the ability to overcome the Jews: but the united Arab effort looked to them like their hope for salvation.

The first shock for Arafat came in the middle of April 1948 when the news reached Cairo of Abdel Kader al-Husseini's death in the battle of Mount Kastel near Jerusalem. He was killed on the night of 7–8 April, and the reaction to his death among Palestinian Arabs was one of deepest emotion. Two days later came the massacre in Deir Yassin. Dissident Israeli military groups (Lehi and Irgun) attacked this Arab village west of Jerusalem, blowing up houses and killing over a hundred men, women, and children. This atrocity was severely condemned by Ben-Gurion and the Israeli leadership, but led to a great flight of Arabs from their homes and provoked a passionate reaction throughout the Arab world.[57]

Hamid Abu Sitta was also a student at King Fouad University in Cairo and information he provides is important concerning what happened then with Yasser Arafat. Abu Sitta was some years older than Arafat and since he was originally from the town of Khan Yunis he knew the al-Qudwa family and Arafat well. He had formerly undergone military training in a small camp set up by Abdel Kader in Syria and had fought for some weeks in Palestine.

When news of the death of Abdel Kader was received, and the defeat threatening the Palestinian Arabs became real, Hamid Abu Sitta convened a meeting of Palestinian students in the club room of the Muslim Brothers. A moving ceremony took place there. Led by Abu Sitta, the students took out their textbooks, notebooks and student cards, and threw them into a bonfire, swearing to stop studying and go fight in Palestine. Yasser Arafat was among them. Then under twenty years old, he was small and thin. Hamid Abu Sitta tried to prevent him from going to Palestine, telling him he had no military experience, but in the end he relented and agreed to take Arafat along on the journey to Gaza.

They set out some days later and arrived at the border in May. Abu Sitta went in the direction of Beersheba and Yasser Arafat apparently joined one of the volunteer units of the Muslim Brothers which on May 10 attacked Kibbutz Kfar Darom, situated not far from Khan Yunis. The attack failed. Less than a week later (on May 15) the unified Arab armies began their invasion. At this time an event occurred which in time would turn out to be one of the most important in Arafat's life. The Egyptian officers, who wanted to conduct a regular war, confiscated the arms of many of the irregular soldiers, including Arafat's. In effect, they threw him off the battlefield.

He went over to the Jerusalem region and stayed there briefly. The same thing happened in Jerusalem. The regular soldiers of the Transjordanian Arab Legion, which was then under British command, hastened to disarm the soldiers of the "Holy Army" (al-Jaish al-Muqadas) which was the local Palestinian army. The former commander of these units in the Jerusalem area had been Abdel Kader al-Husseini, whom Arafat held in such high esteem.

The fact that the commanders and the rulers of the Arab states prevented the Palestinians from fighting of course agitated many, but the anger escalated with subsequent Arab defeats. The shock and embitterment of Arafat and of the Palestinians grew quickly, and over the years, the sense of humiliation which the Palestinians suffered at the hands of selfish, traitorous and corrupt Arab leaders was to serve as a prime motive for Arafat's activity. "The holocaust started when they drove us off the battlefield in Palestine," Arafat and his friends were to say later.[58]

He returned to Cairo, according to his own testimony, depressed and despairing. First he thought of studies in America, then returned to the engineering faculty at the University, where he began political activity within the framework of the Palestinian Students' Association. This Association was unique among student organizations. Membership was on a national (Palestinian) and not an ideological-political basis. The hundreds (maybe more) of Palestinian students studying in Cairo were generally divided in their positions. There were among them fanatical religious people sympathetic to the Muslim Brothers who attacked facilities of the British Army then stationed in Egypt. There were communist cells. Others belonged to groups which backed pan-Arab unity such as the Ba'ath party (which originated in Syria) or the "Arab nationalists" (al-Qawmiyyin al-Arab), an all-Arab movement founded in Lebanon during that period by the Palestinian doctor George Habash. The common country of origin did indeed unite the Palestinian students, but most of the young Palestinians felt greater affinities with those whose political outlooks they shared.

In 1951, at the age of 22, Arafat was not a rank-and-file member of any ideological group but like many others he sympathized with the Muslim Brothers because of their anti-British activities. He underwent, and apparently enjoyed, a short course of military training with a small military reserve set up among the students by the Egyptian Army. Here he acquired knowledge of mines and explosives.

One episode in the autumn of 1951 involving the Palestinian students in Cairo recalled to some extent the anger and humiliation Arafat had felt when they took away his rifle in Palestine and disbanded the Palestinian units. One of the committees of the Arab League decided to do away with the small relief allocation given to needy Palestinian students. There were many of these, mainly the sons of refugees, who had succeeded in being accepted by an Egyptian university. Naturally, they existed with difficulty.

Some dozens of enraged Palestinians broke into the office of Ahmed Shukairy, a Palestinian official then acting as Deputy Secretary of the Arab League and responsible for Palestinian affairs. Among the angry students was Salah Khalaf (Abu Iyad), who was younger than Arafat. The cooperation between them led a year later to their being elected to the leadership of the Students' Association, Arafat as Chairman and Salah Khalaf as his deputy. Following their election, the subject of the allocations to Palestinian students was raised again, and they again conducted a campaign which included strikes, breaking into the Arab League office, and involvement with the Cairo police.

Both in their election campaign among the Palestinian students and in daily activity, Arafat and Salah Khalaf broadcast a very clear message: what is important is that we are Palestinians! Again, this is more important than political leanings, ideology and faith—this is our real common destiny. This approach runs like a dominant thread through Arafat's political career from his war experience in 1948 through his activity among the Palestinian students in Cairo, the establishment of Fatah in the late 1950s, his leadership role in Fatah, and up to the establishment of the Palestinian Authority in Gaza in 1994. The fact that Arafat has been a consistently faithful representative of Palestinian anti-Arab feeling is among the important clues to the riddle of his leadership.

However, a lack of faith in the Arabs and in their ability to unite was not in those early days the accepted message. The new revolutionary regime of Gamal Abdel Nasser preached Arab unity, and Arab unity sparked the imagination of the Arab masses. In Syria the Ba'ath (Renaissance) movement made strides, establishing branches in various Arab countries. Throughout the 1950s and even later, the idea of Arab unity particularly captivated the Palestinians. They were enthusiastic Nasserists, Ba'ath supporters, and leftist revolutionaries. Arafat's brand of Palestinian particularism appeared to them as impotent and lacking broad horizons. What could a small Palestinian movement achieve compared to the great strength latent in Arab power "stretching from the stormy Ocean to the raging Gulf?" in the words of Ahmed Said, the popular broadcaster on the Voice of Cairo.

There is evidence that even then, at the beginning of the 1950s, Yasser Arafat and some of his colleagues had played with the idea of organizing guerilla activity against Israel and that they also persuaded President Nasser to establish special units for this purpose. Actually, only one of them, Khalil al-Wazir (Abu Jihad), who was active in the Muslim Brothers cell in Gaza, tried his hand in the early 1950s in the organization of quick forays from Gaza into Israeli territory. However, he also gave it up, took up studies in Cairo, and in the latter part of the 1950s went to look for a job in the Arab oil states. The Suez Campaign of 1956 (in which Israel attacked Egypt with the assistance of British and French forces) ended with a hasty Israeli retreat as the result of American-Soviet pressure and with an impressive political victory for Egyptian President Gamal Abdel Nasser. The idea of Arab unity under Nasser's leadership was at the peak of its success, leading to the establishment of the "United Arab Republic," the first political union between Egypt and Syria. This pushed aside 'localized' national initiatives (iklimi in Arabic) which were condemned as worthless.

Now in his twenties, Yasser Arafat, who wanted to be Mr. Palestine, was a student official no longer in office, and an engineer searching for a livelihood first in Saudia Arabia and later in Kuwait. The platform belonged to Egypt's President Nasser, who aspired to be Mr. Arab, and to his Palestinian counterpart, Dr. George Habash.

The slogan coined in those days was that the liberation of Palestine emerges through Arab unity. In other words, first the Arab peoples and states must be united and only then will the clenched fist be created which will be able to crush the state of Israel. "Unity—liberation—revenge" was the cry of the National Arab Movement led by Habash. Even though this movement sought to unite all the Arabs, most of its members were Palestinians whose center was in Beirut, with branches in several countries. They opposed the establishment of any specifically Palestinian entity because in their view it would only add to the divisions among Arabs and weaken the trend to unity.

The end of the 1950s was perhaps the lowest point of all in the story of Yasser Arafat and his colleagues who, while continuing to believe in the Palestinian identity, were compelled to give up their activities. They scattered in various directions and contact between them became looser. Among them were teachers, officials, engineers and academics, and they settled in the Gulf principalities, in Jordan and in Lebanon, as well as further afield in European countries. Most of them married and established families. Yasser Arafat, however, who worked in Kuwait, remained single. Rather than constituting any organized entity, these compatriots formed various groups of young Palestinians, mostly academics, who met from time to time to analyze their sad situation. Many established ephemeral and unimportant political organizations.

One such group, numbering five people, set up the Fatah[59] organization in Kuwait in October 1959. The five were the engineer Yasser Arafat, who worked in the Public Works Department in Kuwait, and later along with a few partners established a small contracting company; the teachers Salah Khalaf (Abu Iyad) and Khalil al-Wazir (Abu Jihad), old acquaintances of Arafat; Farouk Kaddoumi (Abu Lutf) who found work in the Kuwait Health Deparment; and Khaled al-Hassan (Abu Said), son of a refugee family from Haifa and a government official in the Ministry of the Interior, who managed to attain a high position and even to receive Kuwaiti citizenship. Within a short time a few other young Palestinians from Arab countries joined them, of whom the most outstanding were three men from the Principality of Qatar: Mahmoud Abbas (Abu Mazen), Yousef al-Najjar and Kamal Adwan (the last two were murdered by Israeli commandos in Beirut in 1973).

Their first action was to bring out a small publication called *Filastinuna* (Our Palestine) financed from their own pockets and from the few donations which they managed to collect. It appeared irregularly from November 1959. The publication, which unified the small group, preached the establishment of an independent Palestinian entity. The writers did not sign their own names. Their demand was to start a campaign for liberating Palestine, which they saw as the only way to achieve Arab unity. This stand was contrary to everything then accepted in the Arab world, and even among most Palestinians.

The group and the publication gradually crystallized their positions, demanding that the Palestinians take their fate into their own hands independently, without relying upon any Arab power. The slogan "armed struggle" was also added to their terminology, overshadowing the other slogans. The essence of their teachings was that the Palestinians must set up an authentic national body which would commence military action against Israel. Yet even if the appearance of Fatah attracted some attention in the Arab world and among Palestinians, one could hardly say that the group achieved success in its early beginnings. Indeed, the opposite was true. At least until 1961, separatist stands opposed to Arab unity were totally rejected, as was the call to open a military struggle at a time when the Arabs felt they were not ready to grapple with Israel.

Since we are speaking of a small and peripheral group in the Middle East arena of the early 1960s, it is difficult to analyze its structure and leadership. Its members, mostly as we have noted from Kuwait, occasionally traveled to Beirut where they hired the services of a small office and a post office box, through which they put out their publication whenever they could muster the necessary budget. Yasser Arafat stood out for his enthusiasm and energy and his readiness to invest more time than the others. But like the rest of the Fatah members, he held on to his job. Most had also to look after families. Khalil al-Wazir (Abu Jihad) and not Yasser Arafat, was the first to leave his position in Kuwait in order to become a full-time worker in the organization. Arafat only left his job in 1964.

The turning point came with the disintegration of the United Arab Republic, the Egypt-Syria union, which broke up in September 1961. With hindsight one sees that the political circumstances of the early 1960s created a favorable background for promoting the ideas of Arafat and his colleagues. Only when cracks started to appear in the vision of Arab unity could proposals for separatist Palestinian positions be heard. More and more Palestinians began to take an interest in the views of the obscure Fatah organization, and especially in its demand to launch an armed struggle. This interest made it possible to bring in more members and to establish new cells.

"Until then we had nothing better to suggest than the Muslim Brothers, the Communists or the Arab Nationalists," Abu Iyad was to write later,[60] while in the early 1960s Arafat and his colleagues started to propose "armed struggle" to the Palestinians as something rising over and above all ideologies. Young people joined them as disappointment began to set in with Islamic, Arab, class or international cooperation. It became clear to them that the only real partnership would be that of the Palestinians, "a partnership for the return of the plundered homeland."

From Yasser Arafat's point of view, Fatah and *Filastinuna* were the natural continuation of the path which he had taken since his youth: intensive Palestinian identity, an independent Palestinian army (the 1948 Holy Army), the Students' Association on a separate national basis without "foreign ideas," and now an organization raising only one flag—the Palestinian flag, symbolizing the struggle for liberation of the homeland.

What happened to Arafat and the Palestinians between the years 1960 and 1964, when Fatah was established and set out on its first military action, can be described in one sentence. Rather than the Palestinians having created a renewed identity, their Palestinian identity was forced upon them. With little exaggeration one can say that they had no alternative but to accept Arafat's solution and to be Palestinians.

In the early 1960s Arafat and his people numbered only a few dozen members. They were in their thirties, mostly from refugee families who in their youth had personally experienced uprooting and loss of home. The sons of the "generation of defeat," they had seen their parents conquered in battle and unable to build new homes in the neighboring Arab countries. The revolutionary organization which they established drew its inspiration from the underground in Algeria and from the revolutionary ideologists of the Third World, such as Franz Fanon (*The Wretched of the Earth*). They strove to become "the generation of revenge." From the moment they formulated a political philosophy based on the need to crystallize a united Palestinian entity by means of a violent struggle against Israel, they challenged their whole environment: Israel, the Arab states, the Arab rulers and that ideology of the Arab states which had neglected the Palestinian cause.

Arafat and his group were compelled to maneuver among powerful forces such as authorities which suspected them, parties which rejected them, and intelligence services which pursued them. The first Fatah people therefore adopted the underground ways of persecuted people. They adopted secret names, forged transit documents, changed their appearance and disguised themselves, employing all the tricks of the trade. But they likewise understood the great importance of propaganda and the media. For Yasser Arafat these years also served as an academy for the study of Middle Eastern politics. He was increasingly absent from his work in Kuwait, until finally he left it completely.

In 1964, as the agony of the Palestinians became an increasingly pressing issue, the "Palestine Liberation Organization" headed by Ahmed Shukairy, was established under Egyptian auspices.[61] For Arafat and his people, the new organization appeared to be yet another attempt to avoid finding a solution to the Palestine problem. They resolved to set out on their first military action against Israel. "Not that we harbored illusions that we could defeat the Zionist state, but we considered that we possessed no other means of compelling international public opinion to take an interest in the Palestine problem, and even more than this we aspired to unite the masses of our people in the popular movement which we had established," wrote Abu Iyad.[62]

Yasser Arafat's achievements in the following years were the result of a number of developments, the most important of which was his political orientation and its acceptance by his own people. From the first half of the 1960s and onward, he succeeded in persuading the Palestinians of his credibility as a leader who was faithful to their interests and who identified with their distress, as opposed to the hypocritical treachery of the Arab world. It is perhaps not a coincidence that Arafat's first article in the Palestinian periodical *Filastinuna* surveyed the suffering of the Palestinians in the refugee camps. The caption of one picture showing destroyed Arab houses in Palestine read, "Houses destroyed as a result of the planning of the Arab League in 1948."

This political course was accompanied, as we have seen, by frequent disputes and controversy with the Arab states. These were deliberate, since Arafat's whole political world was built on the foundation of disappointment and embitterment with the "Arab brothers." From his point of view, he was even "anti-Arab" in his repeated demands to the Arab states not to interfere in Palestinian affairs. "We will not accept the custody of those who drove us out," declared the founders of Fatah from the day they began their movement. In one of their first anthems we read: "Here are the heroes returning/after they had been removed from the battle/through the plots of enemies and traitors."[63]

In the eyes of the Arab rulers Arafat looked like a worthless villain, while to the Israelis his organization appeared to be a cruel enemy. Yet not only did these images not harm him in Palestinian eyes, but the very opposite. The residents of the refugee camps from Rafah in southern Gaza to Nahar-al-Bared in northern Lebanon were convinced of his sincerity and accepted him as a symbol. The secret of his leadership was related not only to his controversial personality but also to the political line he had adopted since his youth. Arafat showed great consistency in pursuing this course until political circumstances, between 1965 and 1968, facilitated a breakthrough for him and his movement.

turning point

On the morning of 3 January 1965, one of the workers in the Israeli Mekorot Water Corporation discovered a small explosive charge which had been placed in a conduit in the National Water Carrier in the Beit Netofa Valley, in Galilee.[64] This national project transfered water from the north to the arid south of the country. The charge did not explode and Israeli investigators found tracks leading to Beit Shean and from there to the Jordanian border. This was the first action of the Fatah organization and it followed long months of preparation for the start of the "armed struggle."

From a military point of view this and similar actions which came after it were pretty wretched affairs. A few groups which together numbered no more than a few dozen guerrilla fighters tried to act as an underground in the border areas with Israel: in the West Bank of the Kingdom of Jordan, in the Egyptian-controlled Gaza Strip, and in southern Lebanon. Their military training was meager. The equipment at their disposal was out of date. Even before entering Israel they were compelled to hide from the Arab authorities and to disguise their activities. Many of them were arrested as a result of being informed on by their own comrades.

Yet in political terms these actions had a powerful effect. They shocked the whole region, and in retrospect, the start of the "armed struggle" by Arafat and his colleagues in early 1965 created a new Middle Eastern reality. A widespread network of false announcements and misleading exaggerations accompanied these meager actions for which the new Palestinian leadership, led by Arafat, was also responsible. It is possible to explain Arafat's biographical distortions as being designed to fit him for the role of representative symbol of the Palestinians, but what explanation can there be for the widespread and untrue propaganda which Arafat and his people consistently put out during their years of military activity?

An examination of the data from the first year of the "armed struggle" shows that there were 35 incursions into Israeli territory for the purpose of placing explosive charges and for sabotage against civilian facilities like water pipes and reservoirs. Most of these came from the West Bank of the Kingdom of Jordan, and a few from the Gaza Strip and Lebanon. Dozens of additional actions were prevented by the security forces of these countries, which arrested and imprisoned the underground Fatah units. One fact deeply engrained in the Palestinian memory of those days concerned Ahmed Musa, the first Palestinian to fall, who was leading an early action aimed at damaging Israel's National Water Carrier. He was killed during his retreat, after crossing the Jordan. It was not the Israeli enemy who shot him, but soldiers of the Jordanian army who encountered him on his way back. They demanded that he lay down his arms, and he refused.

These first actions were intended less to harm the state of Israel than to express a protest against the Arab states, a challenge or provocation to the Arab regimes. And it was not only the Arab governments which came out against these actions, but also those Palestinians who believed in Nasserist and pan-Arab ideologies and still pinned their hopes on their Arab brothers. Much of the Arab media which were subject to government supervision, understandably chose either to overlook or to criticize Fatah activities. Of course great prominence was afforded to

Fatah incursions in the Israeli media and the Syrian media did publish the press releases of al-Assifa (the Thunderstorm) which was the underground title of the military wing of Fatah. But Fatah's most important publicity came from Lebanon, which was then the capital of the Arab free press. A stormy debate broke out in the Lebanese media between supporters and opponents of the military-political course taken by the Fatah organization.

Arafat and his people strove to give their military activities an exhibitionist character with protest demonstrations by the Palestinians. They wanted the activities to agitate the Arab public. In this they enjoyed impressive success, achieved in part by a broad campaign of heroic rhetoric.

It started with the publication of "Military Announcement No. 1" which spoke of "storm troops which moved into the conquered territory in order to open the struggle against the enemy." There followed scores of items about the destruction of dozens of tanks and the killing of hundreds of enemy soldiers.[65] In those days the Fatah leadership retained its anonymity. People neither identified themselves in public nor appeared in press conferences nor were interviewed in the media. But they promulgated a growing flood of communiqués on their successful military struggles against Israel. Later Abu Iyad was to say that "we wanted to amaze everyone."[66]

Arab reactions to the first Fatah operations in 1965 confirmed the longstanding political outlook on the "treason" of the Arab brothers. Egyptian spokespeople directed by Gamal Abdel Nasser described the Fatah activities as the deeds of extreme and fanatical Muslim Brothers who received financial allocations and instructions from the Imperialists and the CIA. The Saudis referred to the Fatah as agents of international communism. The Jordanians regarded them as dangerous revolutionaries. Those Palestinians who were close to Arab nationalism also condemned them as irresponsible adventurers, while Ahmed Shukairy, the chairman of what was then the PLO (before Arafat replaced him) called them enemies of the Palestinian liberation movement.[67]

The strong criticism of Fatah's first activities did no harm to the organization. On the contrary, it drew attention to them, strengthened their popularity in the Palestinian public, particularly in the refugee camps, and during 1965 even forced its opponents to change their minds. The Six-Day War in June 1967 broke out to a large extent because Fatah's position that armed struggle must be started against Israel had won many adherents in the Arab world as a whole and among the Palestinians in particular. Ahmed Shukairy pretended to raise his own guerrilla units. George Habash and the Arab nationalists established military units. And above all, Syria and the Ba'ath regime, and Egypt under Gamal Abdel Nasser who was so esteemed by the Arab masses, were dragged into militant activity which finally brought about the outbreak of war and the Arab defeat in 1967.

In six days of battle, Israel thoroughly defeated the Arab armies, capturing Sinai, the Golan and the areas of the West Bank and Gaza. The state of Israel became ruler over more than half the Palestinian people. Facing a bewildered and defeated Arab world, on 23 June 1967 the Fatah leadership under Yasser Arafat held a meeting in Damascus. The decision was made to continue the struggle through transfer of the headquarters to the conquered territories.

At the end of the summer, Arafat crossed secretly into the West Bank, staying there for several weeks. Though he was not famous, his name was already known to Israeli Intelligence and a number of attempts were made to capture him. He moved from one hiding place to another, helped by the underground cells whose organization in the West Bank had begun. He spent most of his time in the areas of Nablus and Ramallah, where he organized a network of activists.

These weeks saw full expression of his courage and acting ability. He changed his disguises, used forged documents (Israeli identity cards had not yet been issued to the population) and frequently traveled by bus. Stories of how he evaded IDF soldiers, how he managed to walk the streets of Tel Aviv, and even passed several times back and forth to eastern Jordan—all these became an important part of the myth of heroism and survival associated with Arafat.

Only after Arafat left the West Bank in autumn 1967 did the first sabotage operation in the conquered territories begin, in accordance with the doctrine of "popular struggle" which the Fatah leadership had adopted. The propaganda campaign which accompanied the action grew increasingly louder. At the start of 1968 the Israeli security forces succeeded in capturing many of the Fatah underground cells in the occupied territories, and anti-Israel underground activity was pushed further and further eastward, to the Jordan River border. To the east of the river the Palestinian organizations set up headquarters centered in the township of Karameh. In March of 1968, in its first extensive action since the Six-Day War, the Israeli army attacked Karameh, by that time almost deserted by its civilian population.

Arafat was then in Karameh. In emergency debate with Palestinian commanders there, he insisted that they must not retreat. His opinion was accepted, and indeed the Israeli army action ran into trouble. The IDF soldiers did not succeed in taking the Palestinians, who hid in caves in the vicinity. Meanwhile, Jordanian armored vehicles interfered in the battle and knocked out several Israeli tanks. The battle ended with an Israeli retreat, and a Palestinian victory celebration followed in which the whole Arab world took part.

A few days after the Karameh battle, Yasser Arafat's name became publicly known. An official announcement of the Central Committee of the Fatah organization called him the official spokesman of the organization and authorized him to be the only one entitled to publish announcements in the name of Fatah. In Fatah's internal circles and in the intelligence services of the states in the region, his name had of course already been known. But the fact that his was the first name to be divulged to the public, and the timing of this revelation along with the Karameh action, were of great importance. April 1968 was the date when the enigma of Arafat first began to grow: a leader enshrouded in mystery, who always appeared in the same military uniform, with streaks of beard, dark glasses, a kaffiyeh and a Kalashnikov, was linked in the consciousness of the people with what Arafat defined as the "first historic victory of the Arabs against the state of Israel."[68]

The political circumstances of those days pushed Arafat forward within a few weeks to the status of a singular hero. Against a degraded Arab world which had just the previous summer absorbed a terrible blow in the Six-Day War, suddenly the man who symbolized the restoration of downtrodden Arab honor took his stand. Palestinian publications spoke of the heroic battle and victory of Karameh as carrying equal weight with the Israeli victory over the Arab armies less than a year before. The Arab armies had hundreds of thousands of soldiers, legions of armor, planes and advanced military equipment. Yet they could not overcome Israel—until the arrival of Arafat's bold fighters. These, isolated and lacking all the necessary means, nevertheless had beaten the enemy in a battle which Arafat called "a second Stalingrad."[69] And who were the anonymous heroes? Those wretched Palestinians whom the Arab world had neglected and repudiated.

The Arab peoples as a whole, and especially the Palestinian population, needed some spark of hope, someone symbolizing a prospect for change, and Arafat filled this role. After Karameh, thousands of young Palestinians started to stream into the Fatah headquarters in Jordan and the few training camps which existed in other Arab countries. For the first time since taking up political work, Arafat became a leader of masses. What he called the mighty victory of Karameh played a decisive role in this change.

We have seen that even before Karameh, official Fatah announcements disseminated exaggerated and distorted reports of successes against the Israelis. Then it was a question of a small group of Palestinians who were trying in any way possible to get through to the Arab and Palestinian public and to hostile political circles. The exaggerations were a kind of self-promotion by the leaders of the new Palestinian organization who wanted to say: Look, we Palestinians have started to act on our own, we are taking our fate into our own hands without any help from our great and strong Arab brothers.

Perhaps these exaggerations are characteristic of an organization emerging from infancy, like a small child trying for the first time to stand on its own feet. This tendency for exaggeragion, which found its fullest expression regarding Karameh, was compatible with the political line of Arafat and his associates. They were striving primarily to demonstrate their independence, their uniqueness and their heroism as Palestinians, against the indifference of the corrupt Arab regimes which had forsaken them.

After Karameh, during the years 1968–1969, this trend reached its peak and now was assisted by the media in all the Arab states. Joining the ranks of the Palestinian victory march helped to compensate for the Arab defeat of 1967. Thus, a great part of the Palestinian actions and victories reported in this period never actually took place. In March 1968, for example, Israeli Defense Minister Moshe Dayan was injured in an accident while taking part in an archaeological dig near Tel Aviv. A fictitious Fatah announcement claimed that their people had attacked him. Later, when Israeli Prime Minister Levi Eshkol died from heart failure after a long illness, Fatah announced that they had killed him!

Just after Yitzhak Rabin completed his duties as IDF Chief of Staff, Fatah announced that it had blown up the garage where his cars were kept. Actually, Rabin never had a garage.[70] Fatah was quick to take responsibility for a range of chance accidents, fires or other disasters in Israel. In the summer of 1968 five Israeli reserve officers were killed in a road accident near Tel Aviv and again the Fatah spokesperson (Arafat) announced that this was not an accident and that Israel was concealing the killing of these soldiers by Fatah fighters. In this case journalists objected to Arafat that their investigation showed it had indeed been a road accident, to which he responded scornfully: "There has recently been an increase in road accidents in Israel."[71]

Partly or even largely untrue, Arafat's PR campaign was not conducted in a vacuum. A series of political developments helped to create and support it. Now that the Palestinians and the Arab world had finally recognized the presence and power of Palestinian consciousness (that is, Fatah and its ideas) other organizations similar to Fatah were also established. Some were relatively large like the Popular Front for the Liberation of Palestine (PFLP) led by George Habash, which continued along the course of Arab nationalism, or the Democratic Front for the Liberation of Palestine (DFLP), which split from Habash under the leadership of Nayef Hawatmeh, and the Saiqa organization which was under Syrian patronage. To these one must add dozens of small sectarian organizations, which sought to copy the success of Arafat and his people.

All these competed in claims for the number of actions carried out against Israel. This competition resulted in gross fabrications and exaggerations, all intended to flatter the organization concerned and make it look stronger against its competitors. Naturally, every Arab country directed the media according to its own interests. Arafat's announcements on the heroism of his fighters and on their successes, even if they were imaginary, appeared as something akin to sacred writings in the eyes of the Arab public. Since it was forbidden to doubt or deny such revelations, anyone daring to call things into question was considered a collaborator with Israel. The Arab masses and the Palestinians as a whole willingly swallowed Arafat's hyperbole, perhaps even encouraging him to announce more and more tales of heroism. This he did with commendable ability.

Here and there criticisms were heard of the lack of credibility in the announcements of Fatah and its leaders, but the gain from the exaggerated publicity was greater than the loss.[72] Droves of volunteers continued to flock into the Palestinian movement. Its political status soared. Less than a year after Karameh, Fatah and Arafat took over the PLO. Financial contributions and assistance from the Arab states began to pour into the organization's treasury. The accumulation of arms in large quantities began. The international community also started to take an interest in the Palestinians. Suddenly they acquired a political identity and a national character, no longer appearing as a miserable refugee population in need of humanitarian assistance. The person symbolizing all this in his appearance, behavior, and way of life, was Yasser Arafat.

The lack of credibility and truth did not harm Arafat. Throughout his career this has been his style of work to one degree or another. He added to the 1970 civil war in Jordan between the Palestinian organizations and the Jordanian army a bitter campaign of invective against the Jordanian regime. The harm done to the Palestinians in this period was blown up to horrendous proportions. Exaggeration also characterized most of Arafat's anouncements during the long period when he stayed in Lebanon. In 1982 the Israeli army invaded Lebanon in order to fight the Palestinian organizations, and bitter battles around Beirut went on for nearly three months. In the end Arafat was forced to evacuate his forces from Lebanon and to move to Tunis. He did not admit his failure, describing the Lebanese war thus:

> As I took my stand against 169,000 Israeli soldiers in Lebanon, I recalled a discussion I once had with Gamal Abdel Nasser,

who doubted our military strength. Nasser said: "Abu Ammar, would that all the Palestinian units could fight against one Israeli brigade. If you would engage one Isreali brigade in a war, it would be enough for me." And what happened in Lebanon? We held out for 88 days against eight and a half divisions of the Israeli army and their whole air force and navy. This means that almost all the Israeli army fought against us. They had only three divisions left along their borders with the Arab states. They had to have one brigade in reserve, which means that only two Israeli divisions were stationed in this period along the whole Arab front with Egypt, Syria and Jordan. Any Arab force could simply have got up and traveled along the road to Jerusalem. And what happened? Nothing. What can a man say about this?[73]

This is a typical extract from Yasser Arafat's words as PLO leader, conveying unfounded information and producing statements, analyses, and commentary all of which could be charitably defined as extremely implausible. This tendency recurs in almost every one of the thousands of interviews which he has given since being elected Chairman of the PLO. A number of experts determined, for example, that the popular uprising in the conquered territories, the Intifada, which started at the end of 1987, broke out spontaneously, without organization or guidelines from the PLO Command in Tunis. When in an interview I mentioned this to Arafat he reacted with surprise: "The Intifada broke out without the PLO leadership? And what flags and pictures do they raise high in Gaza and Nablus? Your picture?"[74]

Arafat's denial of having supported Saddam Hussein during the Gulf War—though he was viewed on television before millions embracing him—was accompanied by the following explanation: "I did not support Saddam Hussein. All I wanted was to prevent that terrible war, which cost tens of millions of dollars, money with which it would have been possible to feed the whole of Africa and cover most of the debts of the Third World." The same lack of credibility can be seen in remarks he made after arriving in Gaza in the summer of 1994 to start setting up Palestinian self-rule in the conquered territories. He announced offhand the establishment of a port, an airport, and projects for housing and industry, clearly ill-considered and inflated declarations remote from reality.

In Arafat's words there have always been important elements of incorrect information and false interpretation. However, if one scrutinizes them carefully, one discovers that hidden behind the words there is something authentic, close to the reality and the experience of the Palestinian people. In the Lebanon war of 1982, Palestinians did indeed take a stand almost alone against the Israeli army. Arafat concocted incorrect figures on brigades and divisions, but his statement that the Arab armies stood aside and in practice did nothing to assist the Palestinians when the latter were being hit by Israel undoubtedly reflects what actually happened. In regard to the Intifada, it did indeed break out spontaneously but it was supported by a network of popular institutions, students' councils, trade unions and other bodies which had been established over the years by the PLO in the areas of the West Bank and Gaza. One cannot even completely disqualify the reasons he gives for his opposition to the Gulf War. He did support Saddam Hussein, but the mighty resources invested by the United States and the world in that war were out of all proportion to what the international community is prepared to spend combating other centers of evil and suffering the world over.

In Arafat's way of expressing himself, despite all the inaccuracies and exaggerations, there is deep down a certain validity. He speaks to the heart of his people. The purpose of the words is to plot the course along which Arafat has been traveling since his youth. The message is that there exists a Palestinian people, deprived and driven from its land, which is now trying to stand erect and find its rightful place in the region. This people is making a tremendous effort, surging forward, creating precedents, fighting, determined come what may to achieve its goal. He, Arafat, has become their leader and representative: and if there are excesses in presenting the case, they are of no importance whatever because the central problem is so real and the cause so just. Those excesses in presenting the subject have surprised many listeners all over the world, but to the Palestinians themselves they were scarcely relevant.

homeland in a suitcase

Arafat's political activity has included travels so extensive that they became part of his mystery. Among the political leaders of modern times he may well hold the record for world travel. Even people whose professions demand globe-trotting cannot compete with the vast distances which Arafat has covered in his political journeys. In the early days when he was still working in Kuwait, he made many trips to Jordan, Syria, Lebanon and Egypt. Hour after hour he would travel by car, generally with colleagues who were unnerved by his high-speed driving. At least once he miraculously escaped death in a serious accident on the long desert road between Baghdad and Amman.

After his election as PLO Chairman, he began increasingly to fly, so much so that several of his colleagues claimed there were months when he spent more hours in the air than on the ground. "He is not the conventional sort of leader who can only work when seated in their offices surrounded by assistants and body-guards," Rashida Mahran said of him, "but a leader who moves from place to place and is everywhere."[75]

One of his assistants, Akram Haniyeh, who was deported from the West Bank in 1986 and accompanied Arafat on his travels from 1988, said that there was one month in which he visited 45 countries, an average of one and a half countries per day. Haniyeh was so confused that he often didn't know where they were. Everything was mixed up in his head—with the names of cities they were visiting, the people they met, the names of airports, hotels, bedrooms, all becoming parts of the chaos.

For years Arafat and his fluctuating entourage have flown in small executive planes put at their disposal by several Arab states including Algeria, Saudi Arabia, Iraq, and Egypt. In one flight, according to Mahmoud Abbas (Abu Mazen), Arafat remarked while passing over the Indian Ocean that all the states there had recognized the PLO and that they must visit them: the Seychelles, Maldives, Sri Lanka, Mauritius. They would devote just two days to this, after visiting Tanzania. This tempo is routine for Arafat. Hani al-Hassan remembers one journey which began in Saudi Arabia, continued to Bahrain, Iraq, Pakistan, Thailand, China, Bangladesh, India, and back for a second time to Thailand, Pakistan, Saudi Arabia, and Iraq, finishing off with a third visit to Saudi Arabia[76]—and all this in three days!

While Arafat has traveled all over the world, he most frequently visits Arab Middle Eastern countries. For this reason some nicknamed him "the modern Bedouin" who instead of seeking pastures on a camel and a donkey, uses twentieth-century transportation. And like the Bedouin, he and his entourage take with them all they need—phones, computers, modem, and fax machines.[77] Arafat himself and his associates frequently say they are "revolutionaries on a flying carpet."

What is behind these journeys? They involve no trace of enjoyment or sight-seeing, no visits to cultural or historical sites. Apart from some official ceremonies, they have included no festive receptions or cocktail parties, and few official banquets. The whole visit would be devoted to intensive businesslike discussions and to meetings with local Palestinians. During his journeys and even while in the air, Arafat goes on with his daily routine. With the help of his sophisticated equipment, he continues uninterruptedly to receive reports, hold consultations, give orders, and try to ensure that the day-to-day work proceeded just as if he were in his office.

In fact, Arafat needed these endless journeys in connection with his political work. He is a great believer in personal meetings, where the atmosphere can be friendly and even intimate, knowing that in large-scale public events he is extremely unconvincing. His outward appearance has always been unimpressive, his public speaking poor. His embarrassing rhetoric and theatrical behavior frequently appear ridiculous. He has felt far more comfortable in person-to-person encounters, where his real strength lies. Though lacking charisma or magnetism, he has shown an impressive ability in conducting conversation on sensitive issues and has earned a reputation as an agreeable guest and a cordial host. All those who have enjoyed his hospitality have been impressed by his welcoming personal approach, by his personal serving of food to his guests, by his compliments and praise—or on the other hand by his outbursts of anger and, when necessary, of threats. Everything is carefully orchestrated, calculated.

Palestinians who have met him are captivated by the attention he bestows on them and by his interest in their personal affairs. He has an excellent memory and is familiar with the details of all the large Palestinian families, knowing their names, exactly where they live and taking an interest in their work, health, and the education of their children.

In fact, he also encourages stories of personal experiences from everyone. In one of his first meetings with Israeli Prime Minister Yitzhak Rabin in Cairo, he held up the political discussion for some time while he dragged the Israeli ambassador in Cairo, David Sultan, into a discussion on childhood in Cairo. On finding out that Rabin's assistant Jacques Neria was Lebanese-born, he engaged him, too, in personal conversation.

Arafat has sometimes been accompanied in his travels by guests and journalists. One of these, T. D. Allman, gave a dramatic description of one trip, which seemed far more than a routine journey for the purpose of political meetings.[78] In the middle of the night a mysterious voice awakened him in his Tunis hotel and told him to get up: "Don't bathe, don't shave. Run! The plane takes off in ten minutes." He hurried out, accompanied all the time by anonymous voices, in an atmosphere of secrecy and mystery. Even in the plane, when he sat by Arafat, he was not told where they were flying, for how long or when they would be back.

"You're my hostage," Arafat joked with him, as if it was a kidnapping. He pointed out the communications equipment and boasted, "When there is fighting we can send orders within five minutes to the units on the ground." Everything was being done restlessly and feverishly by people who clearly were used to moving constantly from place to place, being forced to take care, to consider every step, to evade being followed, to hide whatever could be hidden and to reveal as little as possible. Hitchcock could not have directed it any better. And these journeys likewise have symbolic value apart from their political purposes. They are undertaken by people who are always compelled to move on. Arafat has traveled endlessly over the years as a sort of allegory of a people who are homeless. His whole life has been a long tale of wandering and this is indeed the essence of the Palestinian experience since 1948. When Arafat left his (temporary) home in Cairo, he first looked for work and moved to Kuwait, then was active in Syria, went on to Jordan, from there to Lebanon, and next fled to Tunis, until he finally succeeded in setting up the Palestinian National Authority which was taking shape in the homeland.

Palestinians everywhere are familiar with the path of suffering of people who lack a homeland and a passport. Whenever he met guests, Arafat liked to put on his regular show, in which he asked his friends and advisers to explain what documents they carry. The answers—an Egyptian laissez passer, a Senegalese passport, a diplomatic passport from the Principality of Qatar, and other temporary documents from Algeria, Morocco, Libya, Honduras, Syria, with renewable visas from Greece, Cyprus, Tunisia, Oman, or Iraq.

Over the years most of the Arab states have been suspicious of the Palestinians and have not permitted them to become citizens in their countries. The Palestinians were compelled to wander from place to place. Only in a few countries like Jordan and Syria were the 1948 refugees received reasonably, on the clear condition that they would not arouse political agitation. In other parts of the Arab world the refugees were made use of as long as they were needed, but whenever they became objectionable they were expelled. This was so in the 1950s, when Egyptian President Nasser forced the Palestinian Council in Gaza, which was under his control, to accept a resolution against Saudi Arabia because of his dispute with the Saudi monarch; the Saudis responded by expelling tens of thousands of Palestinian teachers and officials with their families. This trend continued through 1991, when the rulers of Kuwait expelled 300,000 Palestinians after the Gulf War. Though they had nowhere to go, the Arab states refused to accept them, and thousands waited for long months on the Iraqi border before they gradually dispersed.

The traditional Palestinian family was of an agrarian character and for generations had been based on the extended family unit attached to a village in the homeland. Over fifty percent of marriages among Palestinians take place within the clan, a large part of them with cousins. This is a social structure in which to be wanderers and far from home, with the family disintegrating, is an intolerable punishment. Few Palestinians are unfamiliar with the tale "Men in the Sun," Ghassan Kanafani's story[79] of Palestinian refugees trying to cross the border into Kuwait surreptitiously in search of work. They pay the driver of a water tanker to hide them in the tank. The driver delays his journey in order to chat and joke with the border guards, and the workers die from extreme heat as their hiding place becomes an oven.

Arafat knew this reality well from his early days among the Palestinian students in Cairo in the 1950s. Egypt limited the number of entry permits for Palestinian students from the Gaza Strip. Occasionally they expelled Palestinian students suspected of activity in the Muslim Brothers or the Communist Party. Arafat spent much of his time then running around and pleading for Palestinian students from Gaza to be accepted into Cairo University, and in efforts to prevent the expulsion of others.

The sense of debasement associated with these wanderings, looking for a place to hide, cheating the border guards, pretending to the emigration official that you are not what you are— these are part of the humilation of the Palestinians' life in exile. Moreover, this is precisely what engendered support for the political course proposed by Arafat and his colleagues.

This is, for example, the sort of insult described by Abu Iyad when in the late 1950s he was flying with his wife and small daughter from Kuwait to Egypt. The plane was forced to make a stop in Lebanon, where the Beirut airport security officers refused them a 24-hour transit permit so they could go to a hotel in the city. Instead, they were locked into a small room in the airport. Meanwhile a dog which arrived on one of the flights without the necessary health documents was also put into the little room. "I was consoled by the knowledge that we were not discriminated against any more than dogs," said Abu Iyad. "But not for long: the animal's owners had influence in high quarters and, unlike us, the dog was soon released."[80]

Most Palestinians have stories like this to tell, even those who remained in their homes in the new state of Israel. From 1948 to 1966, the Israeli authorities imposed on those Palestinians who stayed in Israel a military government which obliged them to get permits in order to leave their places of residence. A tale was told of a farmer in Galilee who wanted to sell a cow in a neighboring village and obtained the necessary market permit. However, when

leaving home he forgot his personal permit. He showed the po-
licemen who examined his papers only the permit for the cow, but
overlooking this, they let him go. On the way he reflected happily
how fortunate he was that the police thought he was an animal.

Arafat tells stories of the hardships suffered by even the dead
among his people. When he was in Lebanon, one of his old friends
died while visiting the United States. His wife searched for a
cemetery where she would be allowed to bury him, but couldn't
find one. After extensive inquiry, Arafat found a church in the no-
man's-land between Muslim and Christian Beirut and the funeral
service was conducted there while battles raged all around. Arafat
explained: "We're forced to ask ourselves, where to work? Where
to live? Where to study? Where to be buried? It begins from the
day you are born, and lasts until the day you die. You are born with
nothing—no passport, no address —and then you have no place to
be buried when you die."[81]

Arafat sometimes explains his feverish traveling as due to the
needs of the large Palestinian population spread all over the
Middle East and beyond. The Palestinians understand this. There
hardly exists a Palestinian family which has not been affected by
physical separation. Parents, brothers and sisters, often even cou-
ples, live in different countries, finding it difficult to meet, and
spending a great deal of their time making contact, traveling and
crossing borders. This life is one of constant yearning and home-
sickness. Many Palestinians quote a line from the poet Mahmoud
Darwish: "Is our homeland a suitcase?"

In one of the closed meetings of the negotiating committees
with Israel in 1992, Arafat berated his assistant Bassam Abu Sharif
for submitting an enormous telephone bill for payment. "What's
this, a phone bill for thousands of dollars?" But he at once calmed
down and continued sadly: "What can we do, we are a people of
00—that's our international telephone exchange; how can we
keep in touch without this sort of telephone expenses?"

survival

If Yasser Arafat has entirely submerged his private personality in a public, national persona, then the way to understand his leadership is to uncover those elements in his character which correspond with the components of Palestinian identity. This identity was shaped after 1948, when the Palestinian people were no longer living mainly in their homeland. They were a population defeated by their enemies and betrayed and oppressed by their brothers. In response they developed a new identity as a nation in distress, existing on past memories and fostering illusory plans for the future. The Palestinians were a body of people living in expectation, waiting for "next year, next time,"[82] for something in the future which would correct the injustice, change the ugly and inequitable present, and give the people a square deal.

Until then, they needed to hold out, to survive. And nobody could compare with Arafat as a symbol of the ability to emerge from crises, to escape dangers and death—and to survive, both personally and politically. In one conversation, Arafat counted forty attempts on his life, as well as dozens of occasions when he emerged safely from battles and accidents. He succeeded in hiding from the Israeli security forces when he crossed the Jordan River into the West Bank in 1967 and operated in the underground there for several weeks. He emerged unscathed from the battle of Karameh and the civil war in Jordan, where thousands of Palestinians were killed and wounded. Israeli pursuers in south Lebanon did not get him and neither did the bombing of PLO Headquarters in Beirut during the Lebanon war, nor the Israeli bombing of the Headquarters after it was transferred in April 1985 to Tunis. A survey published in Egypt in 1989 includes an account of an attempt to poison him when on a visit to the Far East, an unsuccessful attempt on his life in Romania, and an attempt to plant a bomb in his plane.[83] One of his bodyguards, Abu Tayeb, told how narrowly Arafat escaped on 6 August 1982, when Israeli planes bombed the al-Sanai building in west Beirut one minute before Arafat was due to enter it.[84] Not only did he elude the efforts of Israeli and Arab agents to kill him, but in 1983 he also overcame a rebellion within his own movement. Innumerable attempts have been made by his enemies to conspire against him and to overthrow him, not to speak of plots by his Palestinian adversaries (the Abu Nidal group) to do away with him. All these efforts have failed. Twice Arafat has been wounded in accidents. The most severe case was when his plane crashed in a storm in the Libyan desert in April 1992. The two pilots and the navigator were killed and Arafat and his companions injured.

Because of all these narrow escapes, Arafat has been called "the cat with nine lives," but he prefers the image of the phoenix, the legendary bird which according to Egyptian mythology arises from the flames whenever it is sacrificed on the altar at Heliopolis. Arafat sees not only his personal fate but more importantly, the fate of the Palestinian people as akin to that of the phoenix, which is reborn from its ashes and which no flames can consume. The Palestinians will repeatedly shake themselves free from their suffering and from attempts to destroy them, and return once again to live together as a people.

Arafat's survival for decades at the head of the Palestinian movement is particularly astonishing in view of the fact that so many of his friends and associates fell during this long march. Among his old comrades, founders of the Fatah movement, he is almost the only one left. Khalil al-Wazir (Abu Jihad), who was his partner in the leadership from the beginning of the movement, was killed in a raid by Israeli Commandos on Tunis in 1988. Salah Khalaf (Abu Iyad), his deputy from the days of the Palestinian Students' Association in Cairo, was murdered in 1991 by someone from Abu Nidal's (Sabri al-Banna) extremist Palestinian terror group. People from Abu Nidal's Revolutionary Council set out to eliminate the entire PLO leadership and since 1978 they have murdered 16 Palestinian diplomats and senior PLO acivists, mainly in Europe. The best-known of these were Issam Sirtawi and Said Hammami. Abdel Hamid (Abu Houl), head of the PLO security services, was among those killed along with Abu Iyad in Tunis.

After the death in Morocco in October 1994 of Khaled al-Hassan (Abu Said), the only surviving Fatah founder other than Arafat was Farouk Kaddoumi (Abu Lutf). Though he has been responsible since the Oslo agreement for the PLO's foreign affairs, his activity has been restricted since the start of the peace process, due to differences of opinion with Arafat.

From the second circle of what is called the "historic leadership" of Fatah, only one person remains, Mahmoud Abbas (Abu Mazen), who also disagrees with Arafat's present methods and is less active than he was. The rest have either resigned, died, or been murdered. One of the first, Mohammed al-Najjar (Abu Yousef) was killed in a secret raid by Israeli soldiers on Beirut in April 1973. Kamal Adwan, a Fatah founder, and Kamal Nasir, the PLO spokesperson, were also killed in this raid. Israeli agents were behind the killing of Ali Salameh (Abu Hassan) as well, a Fatah commander who planned the Palestinian terrorist attack on the Israeli athletes at the Munich Olympics. He was killed by a bomb which exploded under his car in Beirut in 1979. Many Palestinian activists have been killed over the years in clashes with Israel. Many more were killed in battles against Syrian and Jordanian soldiers and in internal clashes between different Palestinian factions.

For many years Lebanon served as a permanent arena for hundreds of murders and political assassinations. During the period when Lebanon was the PLO center, a number of leading Lebanese personalities were killed, including President Bashir Gemayel (14 September 1982) and the Druze leader Kamal Jumblatt (16 March 1977), as well as thousands of activists in underground groups, including many Palestinians. Yasser Arafat escaped all efforts to harm him.

Once, according to an unconfirmed report, an attempt to poison his food was discovered. He said this was done by Israeli agents. On another occasion the convoy of cars in which he was traveling was attacked in the Lebanese Bekaa by agents of Syrian Intelligence. Several of his colleagues were killed but he remained unhurt.

This was not only a matter of luck. Yasser Arafat's way of life has been that of a pursued underground figure who takes constant care not to expose himself. He is always armed and surrounded by numerous bodyguards who even sleep in his room. He often repeats that he has never been accustomed to sleep for more than two or three nights in one place. "I never know where I'll go to sleep" he says. His office staff knows that he only decides on this at the last moment.

His hours of sleep are irregular as well. He goes to sleep at dawn and works at night, when he holds meetings and conferences, as if to preserve his watchfulness in the hours of darkness, when he is most liable to be attacked. One winter day in 1993, Egyptian President Hosni Mubarak phoned and asked him urgently to come to Cairo to meet a group of American Jewish leaders. Arafat said he would arrive at midnight, to which Mubarak replied angrily, "They're not revolutionaries, at night they go to sleep." Arafat said he would try to come earlier and in the end he arrived at 11:00 P.M.[85]

In order to ensure his personal safety, he behaves like someone who must constantly confuse pursuers. He changes his schedule at a moment's notice, taking care to maintain secrecy over his journeys and flights, and changing not only planes and cars but also destinations. A typical example from former years occurred in the arrangements for his flight to New York when he appeared at the United Nations in 1974. Arafat and his staff asked Egypt to prepare a plane at the Cairo airport. A similar request was made to the Syrians and a plane waited for him in Damascus too. In the end Arafat flew to Algeria and from there to New York in a third plane. When they entered American airspace they delayed identifying themselves to the airport authorities for almost an hour after the appointed time. Confusion and changes of schedule also accompanied Arafat's departure from New York. The whole journey had the air of a dangerous adventure. Arafat explained later that "we have no alternative. The entire Palestinian revolution is basically an adventurous activity."[86]

Arafat has used similar methods throughout his career. A recent example is his entry into Gaza in the summer of 1994 in order to take over the Palestinian Authority. The crowds who sought to welcome him had to put up with diversionary activity and confusion: the Egyptians prepared helicopters but the Palestinian security services provided contradictory information on the convoy which would take Arafat from the Egyptian border to Gaza. Even his associates didn't know by which route he would finally decide to come to Gaza. Many of them complain that this sort of disappearance has frequently prevented them from knowing where Arafat is and what he is doing. "How can one attack a man when nobody knows where to find him," said Abu Mazen.[87]

His security arrangements occasionally include strange quirks. The journalist T. D. Allman who accompanied him on one of his journeys relates that after a while he discovered a man on the plane whose role was unclear. He asked Arafat who the man was and he was instructed to identify himself: "I am the Chairman's secret pilot. If any of the pilots try to divert the chairman from his destination . . . to the right or left, I take over the cockpit and make sure that the Chairman goes straight ahead to where he wants to go." When asked his name he laughed and answered, "Many Israelis and Arabs would pay a great deal of money to know that."

In former years Arafat used to disguise himself on his secret journeys. In Palestinian folklore such stories have attained the stature of national legends. In his short stay on the West Bank after the 1967 war, he appeared in several places as a rural teacher, as a *fellah* (peasant) or as a shepherd. He wandered around Jerusalem in the garb of a Muslim sheikh or a Christian priest, or dressed up as a woman. In this way he was even able to enter an Israeli military court in Ramallah and attend the trial of one of his men who had been captured.

Popular tales about him include other admiring details about the sixth sense which he has developed to avoid danger. The elements of the story are always the same: Arafat's sudden decision to leave a certain house or bunker or cave and take up a new hiding place. Soon afterwards, the house/bunker/cave becomes a death trap. The enemy finds them, raids them and blows them up, but Arafat, with his amazing flair, had smelled the impending danger and escaped. In some of the tales he was saved by no more than a few moments. His bed in Ramallah was still warm when the Israelis came to capture him there in 1967. He sped away on a motorcycle on the road from Karameh a few moments before an Israeli helicopter landed there (1968). The Jordanian army attack on his headquarters in Amman was mounted only seconds after he left (1970). A bomb fell on his bunker in Beirut immediately after he had left the place (1982).

Not a word suggesting that he fled in fear is to be found in these stories. On the contrary, Arafat's behavior is always presented as that of a hero wily enough to overcome his pursuers, and his actual history unquestionably justifies an appreciation of his courage. Exploits like his infiltration into the West Bank, the decision to fight in Karameh, the organization of guerrilla activity in southern Lebanon, his persistence against the bombing in Beirut, and the return to Tripoli in north Lebanon to continue the fight—all these took place under the personal direction of Arafat. And the PLO leader certainly knew how negative the impact would be were he ever to appear as a coward fleeing from the battle.

A French journalist[88] tells how one day during the war in Lebanon he was waiting for Arafat at the entrance to the command bunker in Beirut. The area was under heavy shelling when Arafat arrived in his car and noticed journalists and TV cameramen waiting for him from behind cover. He crossed the road ostentatiously to a sidewalk café whose tables were quite empty. On one table stood a chess set. "Who wants to play with me?" Arafat cried out to the journalists hiding from the shells.

More than once Arafat has been asked how he overcomes the fear of a man who knows he is hunted, with the danger of death constantly at his back. The best response was his detailed description of what happened when his plane was about to crash in the Libyan desert in April 1992. The three pilots told him that their fuel was exhausted and they had no alternative but to make a blind crash landing. Arafat, ever conscious of being a national symbol, decided first of all to change his clothes. He took off the sweatsuit he was wearing, put on his military uniform and his revolver, and carefully arranged his kaffiyeh in its usual symbolic form (according to the map of Palestine). Dead or injured, he couldn't allow himself to be taken in casual clothes. After he had changed, his colleagues wrapped him up in blankets and pillows, and had him sit in what they thought was the least dangerous place, toward the rear of the plane. He was quiet and composed. A believing Muslim, he is sure that a person's fate is entrusted to God, who apportions the years of each life. This is religious fatalism inspired by a degree of courage. After whispering some verses from the Koran, he cried out: "Oh Abu Jihad, wait for me—I am coming to join you."[89]

Among all his dead comrades, Arafat chose to call for Abu Jihad, who was the closest of all to him, though on the walls of the entrance to his office in Tunis and in Gaza, and in the offices themselves, Arafat hung up pictures of many others from the historic leadership who are no longer alive. He has surrounded himself on all sides in his daily work by pictures of the fallen, an incessant reminder that he is almost the only one to have survived.

But Yasser Arafat's survival has not merely been the personal affair of someone with luck, or of one who has been unusually astute and careful in regard to appropriate security measures. It has also depended upon the political ability of a leader to preserve his high office against competing adversaries. For decades Arafat has held on to his position as head of the Palestinian national movement in spite of the many attempts to eliminate him and of the defeats he has suffered. On at least three occasions it looked as if he was about to lose that leadership. The first was in 1970–1971 when the Jordanians attacked his people and they fled to Lebanon. The second occurred in 1982 when the Israelis forced him to pull out of Beirut. Immediately after this came the third occasion, in 1983, when a revolt within Fatah broke out against him under Syrian auspices.

For over ten years after that revolt, until 1994, Arafat headed the PLO command in Tunis. For the first time in his life he was far away, a distance of thousands of kilometers (about 2,000 miles), from his people. About half the Palestinians were under Israeli rule and the rest lived scattered throughout Jordan, Lebanon,

Syria and other countries. He had to preserve their loyalty to the
PLO at a time when most were living under regimes hostile to
him and to the Palestinian national movement.

This was an almost impossible mission. Why should they maintain their loyalty to Arafat when he lacked any of the power provided by a state mechanism of enforcement? In their daily lives
they were not in any way dependent upon him, or in need of his
services, for Arafat could provide almost no benefits to sympathizers with his cause. Moreover, in one way or another the
authorities in Israel, in Jordan and in Syria (and to some extent
in Lebanon) repressed any manifestations of support for Arafat
and his command in Tunis, proposing tempting alternatives to the
Palestinians under their control.

The Israeli administration tried in the early 1980s to establish
a political body called the "Village Leagues" in competition with
the PLO. Most of the Palestinians in the West Bank and Gaza
were dependent upon the Israeli economy for their livelihood
and the Israelis exploited this against the PLO. Israeli military law
forbade raising the Palestinian flag. It was illegal to belong to the
PLO and a special law laid down that anyone meeting with a
PLO official would be tried and imprisoned.[90]

On principle, the Ba'ath regime in Syria, with its pan-Arab
ideology, had always denied Palestinian nationality as represented
by the PLO. Those loyal to Arafat were removed from Damascus.
Over the years, President Hafez al-Assad's regime has continued
to sponsor Palestinian groups opposed to Arafat, some of which
pretended to replace the PLO as the representatives of the Palestinians.

The Hashemite regime of King Hussein in Jordan suggested
integration into the Kingdom for the Palestinians, on condition
that they give up their loyalty to the Palestinian national movement represented by Arafat. Most of the residents of Jordan are of
Palestinian origin and a significant portion accepted this proposal.

Under these conditions, it looked as if Arafat had no chance of preserving a Palestinian national unity which would see in him and his leadership the embodiment of their national aspirations.

Yet he succeeded. The reasons are to be found in his perception and expression of the common denominator uniting his people: the longing for national independence in their homeland, Palestine. Ever since he exploded in the early 1960s from the periphery of Palestinian society into the position of PLO leader, Arafat has taken the greatest care to maintain those principles which afforded him credibility and legitimacy. He brought together in the PLO as many streams as possible of the different Palestinian groupings: orthodox Muslims side by side with secular Marxists; nationalist Palestinian Christian Arabs side by side with activists who had worked for the (alien) interests of Arab states; rich capitalists and simple people. The slogans which he coined: "National unity," "armed struggle," "independent Palestinian decision-making," were all accepted as ideas of Palestinian self-liberation which must precede the liberation of the homeland. The agenda was the auto-emancipation of a people which had known defeat, humiliation, wandering, and separation.

Arafat preserved the Palestinian consensus because, in view of the whole course of his life and activity, even from far away in Tunis, he could provide his people with the feeling that without a homeland, the PLO under his leadership was their national home. This was an intangible and abstract homeland, but an honorable substitute, which won recognition by more than 120 states in the world. Through extensive efforts he succeeded in introducing the PLO as member or as officially recognized observer in almost every international organization.

In order to achieve a popular consensus, Arafat had to maneuver unceasingly among the miscellaneous Palestinian groupings. From the beginning he renounced the bestowal of any special privileges on his own organization, Fatah, in the PLO Executive

and institutions. He brought a number of independent representatives into the diverse bodies and allocated positions and offices
even to factions hostile to him. He invested unremitting efforts
into preventing breaches and splits in the organization, exploiting
for this purpose all his ability as a mediator. He conciliated,
threatened, flattered, and tempted the adversaries with money
and office, anything in order to preserve the organizational unity
of the Palestinian movement.

Also renowned outside the bounds of his own movement for
his ability as a mediator, he is very fond of playing the role of
regional arbitrator. For years there was hardly a regional dispute in
which he was not involved: the split between Egypt and Libya
(1975), the Iran-Iraq war (1980), inter-tribal disputes in Yemen
and ethnic conflict in Lebanon. Arafat appeared in every quarrel
with a proposal that he himself should mediate, whether the
American hostage affair in Teheran, or that of the Western hostages
in Lebanon. The role of moderator and intermediary affords the
arbiter prestige and an image of political decency: the Palestinian
entity gained legitimacy from these efforts.

Arafat's political survival has been built on his ability to navi-
gate the course of the Palestinian movement with extreme cau-
tion. In Fatah's internal discussions and in the PLO institutions,
he has permitted almost complete freedom to voice criticism.
Ultimately, however, he almost always succeeds in assuring his
own freedom to act according to his desires. Khaled al-Hassan, a
Fatah leader, who was the first to act as head of the movement's
political department, always said that if a decision was accepted
permitting Arafat to act within a radius of a few inches, he would
convert them into miles.

Arafat always took care not to deviate from the consensus,
however. A researcher who examined the process of decision-
making in the PLO[91] concluded that the consensus itself was
often more important to Arafat than its content. In other words,

if in attempting to move in a certain direction he met strong opposition, he withdrew.

Often he sent up a sort of trial balloon, permitting his associates (the best known was Bassam Abu Sharif) to publish articles or to give press interviews differing in part from the official decisions. Afterward he would examine the reactions and if possible would move the whole Palestinian consensus in the desired direction. He threatened on several occasions to resign, and he only broke the consensus two or three times, on each occasion causing sharp crises and splits in the ranks.

The first case was in 1974, when he put through a decision in the Palestinian National Council (PNC) on establishing an independent national authority over any Palestinian territory that might be liberated. This was the first hint of the possibility of establishing a Palestinian entity alongside Israel—that is, an indirect recognition of the Jewish state. The second instance was at the PNC meeting in Amman at the end of 1984 when an agreement was signed for the establishment of a confederation between Jordan and the PLO. The third came with the signing of the Declaration of Principles with the government of Israel in 1993. The common denominator in all these cases was that Arafat felt each one held the prospect of establishing a basis for a future Palestinian state. The consensus, granting legitimacy to him and his organization, has indeed been dear to him, but not at the expense of delaying the establishment of the state.

Arafat has also been adept at absorbing the sentiments of the Palestinian public and responding to them. At the end of 1990, broad Palestinian public opinion in regard to the Gulf War was shaping up in support of Iraq. Sadam Hussein's provocations of the United States, the linkage he created between his willingness to retreat from Kuwait and Israel's retreat from the conquered territories, his threats and his use of missiles against Israel—all these enthused the Palestinian masses. Arafat was well aware of the relation of forces in this conflict and understood that supporting Saddam Hussein might cause him grave damage (as indeed happened). Had he adopted a position hostile to Iraq, though, he might have forfeited all his prestige and status in the eyes of the Palestinians.

At the outset of the Intifada a confrontational German journalist asked Arafat whether the PLO had organized the agitation and the uprising in the conquered territories. Arafat gave him a sincere and truthful answer: "The PLO and Arafat cannot ignite any fire if the people do not want it." In a way, Arafat was copying the behavior of *The Little Prince* who according to the well-known French fairy tale asks his people what they want to do. When they reply, he orders them: "So do it. That is my order." When the spontaneous popular uprising broke out in the West Bank and Gaza, Arafat commanded the people to go forth into the Intifada.

ascetic image–strange marriage

Yasser Arafat has always lived an austere life with few material requirements. The fact that as a young man he did not marry or build a family or a home enabled him to adopt almost a hermit's lifestyle. He was never a *bon viveur*. The journalists Janet and John Wallach, who interviewed his childhood friends, found that as a teenager he was never accustomed to chase after luxuries, to go to parties, to go swimming in the sea or to go out with girls. They asked him (in 1989) when he had last gone out to eat in a restaurant and he answered that he couldn't be sure, but it was probably after leaving Beirut in 1982. He said that only when he was working as an engineer in Kuwait had there been a short period when he had frequently gone out to enjoy himself. Ever since, for over three decades, Arafat has not led a normal life: no vacations, trips or picnics; no visits to museums, cinemas, theaters, concerts or tourist sites, or any sporting events. Occasionally he has permitted himself to watch childrens' cartoons on TV for a short time, perhaps his only form of entertainment.

All those things which people usually do in their free time have held no interest for Arafat. He sleeps little, his meals are simple. He likes sweet things, especially honey, and these make him put on weight. He generally eats late at night along with his advisers and assistants. One of his associates says that they do everything to avoid his invitations for a meal because the food is bland, and he neither drinks nor smokes, although they permit themselves to smoke in his presence.

Interestingly enough, Arafat has almost no personal possessions. Office and home are for him synonymous. Office equipment, telephones, faxes, radio and television to hear and see news all the time—this is the furniture with which he lives 24 hours a day. In place of a bookcase he has office files. His closet contains only military clothes, the kaffiyeh, a peaked military cap, and a few sweatsuits. On ceremonial occasions he wears a khaki-colored cape above his uniform. In other words, his personal possessions are also accessories of the Palestinian revolution. He owns nothing else.

His staff suggested that he attend the dignified official White House ceremony honoring the agreement with Israel in civilian clothes. He refused. They begged him at least to replace the faded jacket, but after examining it he said: "It's excellent work, what's wrong with it?"

After the agreement, West Bank businessmen came to him for a long and tiring meeting in his new Gaza office. A meal was served and then Arafat whispered something to an assistant. The businessmen were amazed when within a few moments a bed was brought into the room and Arafat prepared for sleep. His guests hurried away.

After his unexpected marriage to Suha Tawil in Tunis in 1990, she spoke of her efforts to make the house/office into a family home. The few rooms looked to her like a neglected barracks, almost without furniture, with weapons in every corner, cigarette stubs and stains from rifle grease on the floor.[92] It is doubtful if she has succeeded in changing a lifestyle much like that of a junior army officer who lives and eats with his men at the front. When a journalist asked Suha if Arafat had courted her, or invited her out to dinner or to go dancing, she answered: "Are you crazy?"[93]

From time to time Arafat has received gifts from guests or heads of state, but these do not seem to have impressed him much. One of the secretaries in his office says that there were times when he hardly even looked at them. But his austere lifestyle has also been put, of course, to good political use. After one of his meetings in Moscow, his hosts tried to drag him to a festive performance of the Bolshoi ballet. This was a usual part of the official program for visitors to the USSR. Arafat was almost persuaded but withdrew at the last moment. "What will they say in the refugee camps if they see me spending my time in this way?" he asked.[94]

Sometimes Arafat and his entourage have tended to exaggerate in describing his modest lifestyle, knowing the positive impression this makes in Palestinian public opinion. The dozens of journalistic features on his unusual life and his lack of home and family always carried the message that this is no coincidence, for it is the Palestine Liberation Organization which is his home and all Palestinians are his family.

Over and above this, Arafat has exploited his asceticism to control his associates, most of whom have families and lead normal lives. These people needed money, and the PLO was for many years a very rich organization because of regular financial allocations from the Arab states and in particular from the oil states. According to a decision of the Arab League, the oil states deducted a certain percentage of the salaries of their Palestinian workers for the PLO.

This financial plenty enabled the PLO to set up a large official apparatus, to maintain military units in camps from Libya to Yemen and Iraq, to establish a welfare system for families of prisoners, the fallen and the wounded in the West Bank and Gaza, to open over a hundred diplomatic legations all over the world and also to invest in maintaining health and education services in the occupied territories and in Palestinian concentrations in Lebanon. With the help of these funds, the PLO became affluent, and the newspapers and radio stations at its disposal were integrated into the great propaganda machinery of the Palestinian movement.

Over the years, however, wasteful habits spread in the PLO machinery. The organization lacked efficient supervision of monetary expenditure. Most of the authority for confirming expenses was concentrated in Yasser Arafat's hands. Among many observers an impression was created that Arafat treated with indulgence the wastefulness and corrupt habits of many of the central activists of the organization. His opponents, and especially the spokespeople of opposition groups, as well as Syrian sources, repeatedly described the corruption and the theft of public money. They spoke of dubious deals which were transacted with Arafat's approval. Everyone meeting the leaders of the organization and its representatives the world over noticed their luxurious lifestyle, residing in opulent apartments like millionaires, dressing grandly, traveling in expensive cars, and often being seen in costly restaurants, clubs and vacation sites. Their children were sent to prestigious schools in Europe and America. When they arrived for conferences and meetings, the PLO people stayed in the best hotels along with a train of attendants.

Arafat was of course aware of all this, but instead of trying to fight against the waste and corruption, he appeared even to encourage it. Some said that he was profligate with public money. Many drew the conclusion that Arafat was in fact promoting the corruption all around him. The more the officials surrounding him appeared like corporate managers enjoying a corrupt lifestyle, the more his own asceticism and modesty stood out. He appeared to be a symbol of integrity, deserving of moral superiority over his colleagues in the leadership.

Sometimes he would hint at this disparity to his advantage. In meetings with his people during the night, when most of them were tired and wanted to stop the discussion, he would come out with remarks like: "I understand that you want to hurry to your homes and families and that you have other business to attend to. I have no such thing, and I shall continue to work here. But don't come to me afterward with complaints that I didn't consult with you and that I made the decisions alone."

Similarly he declared on numerous occasions that he did not marry because he was wedded to the Palestinian revolution or nation. He naturally stopped saying this after his secret marriage to Suha Tawil, but Arafat never did announce his marriage officially, either in person or through spokespeople. The information was leaked through the Tawil family almost a year after the secret marriage ceremony took place in Tunis.

The marriage stands in contradiction to the image of the leader and the symbol of Arafat. The fighter who abstained from worldly pleasures, wholly devoted to and identified with the Palestinian revolution, has generally been portrayed as a man without any private life, personifying the collective Palestinian image by erasing his personal identity. Now he has taken a step which is the very opposite of what one could expect from him, marrying a woman with a smart appearance, 34 years younger than himself.

The enigma of Arafat also includes his intimate relations with women. Over the years, the fact that Arafat was known as a bachelor until he was middle-aged gave rise to waves of different rumors. Some said that he had married secretly in the past. At least one source had it that he had even been married and divorced twice. One of these latter women was supposed to be Najla Yassin, of Syrian origin, who had formerly been married to a Palestinian. Since the early 1970s, she had been Arafat's personal secretary and was close to him in Beirut and Tunis.

In the first biography written about him[95] there were repeated hints that he was homosexual. This book even recounts in mocking tones how in the days of the Second World War Arafat, a pudgy fourteen-year-old, served as a homosexual object for his commander in a tent camp near Gaza. According to the book the commander, Majid Halabi (Abu Khalid) wouldn't permit anyone to sleep with Yasser Arafat since the boy was his exclusive plaything and protégé.[96]

Years later, when President Nicolae Ceauşescu's regime in Romania was overthrown, stories were put out by the commander of the president's bodyguard about Arafat's visits to Bucharest. Ceauşescu was said to have supplied him with young male prostitutes, with whom he conducted a stormy homosexual orgy.

None of these stories appears based on any solid ground. They were spread by Arafat's opponents, especially Israeli and Syrian sources. At least one standard biography of Arafat is replete with such lies and aspersions, supported as far as one can tell only by those out to discredit Arafat. One way to examine these phoney accusations is to look at the mass of hostile material published by his Palestinian opponents, especially the people of Abu Nidal's organization. Sabri al-Banna (Abu Nidal) was among the first of the Fatah members to rebel against Arafat's authority. He left in 1973 and set up a rival group under Iraqi auspices. Over the years, Abu Nidal's people killed more than 20 central Fatah activists, including Salah Khalaf (Abu Iyad), Arafat's deputy (in Tunis in 1991). Their hatred of Arafat and his supporters, and of their political course, was unlimited. Their publications relied upon the vast amount of internal information in Abu Nidal's possession and included details of alleged lies, fraud, thefts and personal corruption on the part of many people in the Fatah leadership, including Arafat. In all this wealth of negative material there is not a single word about Arafat's being homosexual. Yet there is no doubt that had Abu Nidal had any information whatsoever on Arafat's sexual habits, he would have had no hesitation in publishing it in order to accomplish the political destruction of the PLO leader.

What, then, gave rise to these rumors? In popular Arab-Muslim culture, the condemnation of adult homosexual activity is extremely strict, and this public morality in turn provides an opportunity for political sabotage. One example of this occurred in 1990–1991 in Tunis, when the authorities arrested leaders of the al-Nahada fundamentalist movement. The government was able subsequently to discredit them by distributing video cassettes showing one of the prisoners engaged in sexual relations with a boy, who had been sent into his cell deliberately to seduce him. It appears that Arafat's opponents, in Israel and Syria especially, attempted to exploit public feeling by using disinformation along similar lines to damage his prestige.

For Arafat's supporters, on the other hand, his reputation as a bachelor served to consolidate his political image as a national symbol. Here and there Arafat admitted that in his private life he had had romances and disappointments. Generally speaking, both he and his associates avoided dealing with the subject and answered questions with words to the effect that he had no time for such things, that there was no place in his world for a woman and a family, that in Abu Iyad's words, "he was torn in younger days between his wish to marry and the fear that he would not find the necessary time for a wife and children."[97] His brother, Dr. Fathi Arafat, has said that as a brother he would like Arafat to have a family but as a Palestinian he wants all the leader's time to be devoted to the nation.[98]

Journalists who put pressure on his assistants and staff heard from them that Arafat was very shy in his relations with women and that there had been a time when he was hurt by women who refused his marriage offers. They would joke about the subject, saying how they wished he would find someone to sleep with at night so that they too could get some sleep. Arafat himself constantly repeated the clichés about all Palestinian women being his women and all Palestinian children his children. More than once he swore that he hadn't married because he was already married. "To whom?" asked the journalist Oriana Fallaci. He answered: "To a woman whose name is Palestine."[99]

This public rhetoric notwithstanding, available information indicates that there were at least two important women in his life before his marriage. Alan Hart, who wrote a semi-official work on Arafat's life, does not mention them in the first edition of his biography *Terrorist or Peacemaker?* (1984). One may assume from this that Arafat and the PLO leadership were rather anxious to avoid the subject.

It was only in later years that more details gradually became available on these two women. The first was Nada Yashruti, who was married to one of the original Fatah people, Khaled Yashruti, a prosperous engineer and contractor in Lebanon (his name appears as one of the first Fatah members).[100] He was killed in Beirut in 1970 in a work accident on a building site when a sack of concrete fell on his head. The widow Nada, who was deeply involved in Lebanese politics, was thought to be close to then Lebanese President Suleiman Franjieh. She served in the role of mediator between Arafat and Franjieh, and Arafat hinted on several occasions that Nada Yashruti was the love of his life.

When the romance became known within the PLO, stories about Arafat having had a hand in her husband's work accident naturally began to circulate. This, too, is almost certainly a false accusation. Palestinian gossip, which may have been correct, claims that Arafat did indeed propose marriage to her but that she rejected him, saying "I love you as a leader but not as an ordinary person."[101] In any case this chapter ended when Nada, returning home from a mission to the Lebanese president in May 1973, was waylaid and shot to death by an unknown assailant. Arafat mourned her for a long time, but during his years in Lebanon he had other short romances. It was also then that he met the beautiful Egyptian writer and lecturer in Arabic Literature, Dr. Rashida Mahran, who became one of his great admirers.

The two became very close to each other after Arafat consolidated his position in the PLO headquarters in Tunis. The relations between them can be studied in a book by Mahran about Arafat, published in series form in the Gulf press (Al-Rai Al-Am, end of 1986 and beginning of 1987). The book is called *Yasser Arafat, a Key Personality,* and the whole work is a hymn of praise to the great leader. Beginning with the introduction, Rashida Mahran writes like this about him: "Whenever I stand before him, trembling all over, I can't control myself, my whole body says love, honor and submission to the leader."[102] Later she hints at intimate relations with him and she tells how she thought she must hurry to Arafat's office/house in Tunis, which she had already described, after it was bombed by Israeli planes on 1 October 1995. "I was afraid of running to the place which was Arafat's office . . . to his bedroom; I still remember all its details, even the tiniest ones, I had spent not a little time there."[103] It turns out that the reason she wanted to reach Arafat's residence was that she had left an envelope of documents there and feared they had been lost in the bombing. But Arafat was in another part of Tunis and not in the house which was bombed. On meeting Mahran he smiled and said: "You'll be surprised to hear that they brought me the envelope which you left with me almost unharmed. The explosion blew it out of the house onto the beach, where they found it. It was saved from the fire which broke out there."[104]

Mahran testifies that more than once she spoke to him about his not getting married. All the world leaders had women who loved them in their lives, why should he be different? The conclusion reached by both (and perhaps this is the reason that the relations between them never reached the marriage stage) was that no woman could be by his side "when his home is a suitcase traveling from place to place on the seat of a plane."[105]

On 22 July 1987, soon after the publication of Rashida Mahran's book, the well-known Palestinian cartoonist Naji al-Ali was mysteriously murdered in London. The killer, who shot him in the morning hours in an alley leading to the offices of the Arab newspaper *Al-Qabas,* was never apprehended. But reliable information reached the British security services that this was an action of the PLO and Fatah apparatus. The murder almost certainly took place in connection with the bold cartoons published by al-Ali.

Naji al-Ali was the son of a refugee family from Galilee who grew up in a refugee camp in Lebanon. He was thought to be close to the PFLP, headed by George Habash. After drawing cartoons for the press in Lebanon and the Gulf, in 1984 he went to work for the international Arab edition of the Kuwaiti paper *Al-Qabas* published in London. His work, which was extremely popular, was characterized by a clear political line criticizing the PLO leaders for leading a life of waste, luxury, and corruption at the expense of the wretched and hungry Palestinian refugee. These leaders always appeared in his cartoons as a fat and debauched gang, holding their meetings in luxury hotels and emptying the pockets of the poor refugee. In one of his cartoons a fleshy politician asks the shriveled, bent, forgotten refugee—Are you from Fatah or a Communist? And the refugee replies—I am hungry.

In his cartoons Arafat was also depicted in a negative light and derided as the principal leader of a corrupt apparatus. It was hinted that one could reach this apparatus through Rashida Mahran's bed. It is difficult to know whether Arafat knew of, or perhaps even gave the order to carry out, Naji al-Ali's murder. However, there can be little doubt that his people committed it. The PLO could not afford to have one of the most sensitive mainstays of their political work undermined.

The ascetic image of Arafat as totally devoted to the Palestinian revolution was an incomparable source of strength for them. The myth of how the leader lived for years with his men in caves in the hills, how he worked unceasingly, sleeping only for a few hours on the floor of his office in Tunis—all this served not only Arafat but also all his associates and the people of the apparatus of the Palestinian movement. They had to portray their movement as clean and unsullied, and as guided by the highest moral criteria. But al-Ali's cartoons set out to destroy all this, presenting a completely contrary picture, one of a depraved gang of wealthy people living a luxurious life of harlotry, and led by Arafat and his Egyptian beauty Rashida Mahran.

Against this background, the question of Arafat's marriage to Suha Tawil is even more perplexing. She was born in 1963 to a Christian family. Her father, Daoud Tawil, was an affluent banker who worked in Jordan and in the West Bank. Her mother, Raymonda, was a daughter of the Hawa family in Acre, who owned property in the Haifa region. When she was young Raymonda, who grew up in the 1950s in the state of Israel, went to live in Jordan and the West Bank.

After 1967 she became well known as an important political activist in the territories. The fact that such a beautiful woman constantly met with foreign journalists and Israeli personalities and demonstrated against Israeli rule did not serve to create an honorable image for her in the eyes of the traditional West Bank and Gaza society. In 1980 she was placed under house arrest by the Israeli authorities, wrote a book on the sufferings of the occupation,[106] and became a media star. Growing up in Ramallah (north of Jerusalem), her daughter Suha was aware of the political activity of her mother, who opened a press bureau for the PLO in east Jerusalem.

From her childhood Suha had known the name of Yasser Arafat, the leader and the symbol who was adored in the household. At the age of eighteen she went to study in Paris where her elder sister, who was to marry Ibrahim Sus, PLO Ambassador to France, lived. In 1984 Raymonda Tawil and her husband also left their Ramallah home. She opened another press bureau supported by the PLO in Washington, living by turns in France and in the United States. Through her mother's activity, Suha met

Arafat in 1987–1988, and in 1989 she helped for a number of days in the preparation for his visit to Paris. He then suggested that she come to Tunis to work in his office there. She agreed, arriving at the PLO headquarters in October 1989.

Soon afterward, gossip started among PLO activists that the two were lovers, and less than a year later, in the summer of 1990, they were married in a secret ceremony in Tunis. Arafat was then 61, Suha 27. The marriage was kept completely secret. The Christian Suha was converted to Islam "for political purposes" in her definition.[107] Apart from the Muslim Kadi, three witnesses, and a small group of confidants, for over a year nobody heard of the marriage.

When the news did come out, the marriage was generally looked upon as strange. It was Suha who had pursued Arafat and initiated their relationship and their marriage. Her father and her mother, Raymonda Tawil, were strongly opposed, and did not always know what was happening. Arafat, by now no longer young, was alone in the top leadership, after most of his comrades from younger days, the Fatah founders, had been killed, had died, or had moved away from him after withdrawing from political life. Those who remained, especially Mahmoud Abbas (Abu Mazen) and Khaled al-Hassan (Abu Said) led a widespread campaign against him. The marriage disgusted them.

Arafat, too, understood the great political damage which could result if his marriage was revealed. For decades now the propaganda of the Palestinian movement had been centered on the image of the fighting hero, alone and homeless, with his unvarnished and spartan appearance, symbol of the Palestinian revolution. Now, suddenly, he marries a young woman with enchanting looks, fair-skinned, with brown eyes and flowing chestnut hair, elegantly dressed in the best outfits of Parisian fashion houses. To add insult to injury, she was a Christian and from a world not only of French museums and cultural events but also of coffee houses, discotheques, and stylish beaches.

The ambitious Suha forced herself on the PLO leadership. They were compelled to give in to her when Arafat refused to reject her, but it was decided to keep the marriage secret in order to minimize the damage. In the end it was Suha's family who finally leaked it to the press.[108] They found it hard to live with the gossip and jokes which went the rounds of the PLO activists about the pretty mistress the leader had found for himself. At least one instance is known of a long dispute, accompanied by shouts and threats, between Raymonda Tawil and Yasser Arafat in his Tunis office.

Even after the marriage was leaked to the media at the beginning of 1992, no authorized announcement by Arafat and his office was ever made. Arafat refused to speak on the subject and he has hardly referred to it in the whole period since then. On the other hand Suha has given press interviews and even published a booklet called *My Life with Arafat* (in Arabic, published by Al-Yarmuk, Ramallah, 1993). Among her statements one can find declarations like "it wasn't he who married me, but I who was joined to him."[109] One of Arafat's closest assistants put it a bit differently when he said that "she married him but he didn't marry her." On the few occasions when they have been interviewed together and asked why they married, Arafat replied: "That's fate," while Suha corrected him and stated, "It's not fate, it's love."

It appears that Arafat's way of life has hardly changed in the wake of his marriage. The husband, his assistants, and his staff did not permit the wife to make many changes, even in the furniture of their joint house/office.[110] The PLO leadership continues to struggle against her. After Abu Mazen announced that he would boycott the ceremony if she participated, she was not permitted to travel to the White House in September 1993 for the magnificent official ceremony marking the signing of the peace agreement with Israel. She has been absent from other official events like the ceremony in Cairo in May 1994 when the details of the agreement were summarized, and Arafat's flamboyant entry into Gaza and Jericho. She came to Gaza several weeks afterward.

They seem to spend little time together. Arafat has maintained his busy routine. His wife does not always know his schedule and may come to his office only to discover that he is out. Even if the whole affair had sometimes looked like a fluke, a momentary manifestation of weakness by Mr. Palestine, it is the exception which proves that all men are flesh and blood. And in December, 1994, it was divulged that Suha was pregnant.

waiting for the chairman

Many of those who have met Arafat, including statesmen, delegates from all over the world, and journalists—not to mention representatives of his own people, the Palestinians—have been charmed by his gracious behavior. While the media image portrays a tough military leader who is not averse to using terrorism as a weapon, who is unshaven, armed and wears battledress, they found to their surprise a small man, gentle, delicate, and extremely well-mannered. They noticed that he always welcomes his guests courteously, opening the door like a gentleman, inviting them in warmly, and taking pleasure in offering them modest meals.

When I met him for the first time in Tunis in 1993, I too was surprised when Arafat hurried to rise from his place at the head of the conference table in order to greet me and my two colleagues from the newspaper *Ha'aretz*. He shook hands warmly and appeared to be excited about the meeting, for which he said he had waited a long time. He subsequently revealed familiarity with my writings over the years and flattered me with praise for my book on the Palestinian refugees.

After three hours of discussion, we moved into a nearby room for supper, with Arafat behaving like a perfect host. He filled our plates, recommended one food or the other, and even spread our bread with fatherly care, telling us how tasty it was.

All his acquaintances confirm that Arafat's personality includes a strong desire to please his guests. One of his colleagues from the Students' Association in Cairo in the early 1950s has related how a Palestinian woman from Gaza once came to them with a complaint that the Egyptian authorities were not permitting her daughter, a student, to go from the Gaza Strip to her studies in Cairo. Arafat assured her that the matter was settled and she left the office content. A member of the Association who was present asked Arafat why he had done this. Why had he given the woman this assurance, even though nothing was in fact settled? Arafat replied that it was difficult for him to see the woman's suffering. He would try to help her and perhaps he would succeed; meanwhile let her go home happy.

Unfortunately, this sort of empty promise has been very characteristic of him. In the early months of his rule in Gaza he handed out such pledges generously to all callers. Merchants and fishermen asked him about plans to build a port and he replied that it would be built within a few months. Farmers inquired about the possibility of exports by air and he promised to build a large international airport within a short time. He likewise promised a speedy solution to housing problems and made a proposal to start immediately with the building of an additional floor on every building in Gaza. To suggestions that these problems are not so simple and can't be solved offhand, he replied "Don't tell me fairy tales. I'm an engineer and I'll look after it personally."

It stands out that one of the characteristics which brought him to the top has been an unremitting daily work schedule of sixteen hours a day, seven days a week, decade after decade. There has never been a report that Arafat, "the dynamo of the revolution"[111] has taken even one day's vacation, and he is hyperactive to an extreme degree. One can sense this in meetings with him when he constantly moves restlessly about in his chair. In an interview in the Egyptian weekly *Al-Musawwar* (November 1989) he was asked "What do you do in your free time?" After looking surprised and almost as if he failed to understand the quesion, he replied: "I know of no such thing." Later he said that in his youth he enjoyed horseback riding, which was his favorite sport. Nowadays he has become accustomed to doing daily physical training exercises according to a system adopted by the Swedish air force.

His vigorous work habits have left no room for the conventional word "schedule." Salah Khalaf (Abu Iyad) who worked alongside him for decades said that Arafat always arrived late in every place and for every meeting.[112] However, being late often helped him. When as students he and his colleagues organized demonstrations in Cairo, Arafat would arrive late, standing well back in the crowd and thus avoiding arrest.

The fact that people have been forced to wait for a meeting with him for hours or days, and sometimes even weeks and months, however, can drive his assistants mad. Some have tried to explain that the deliberate disorder in Arafat's schedule is a security precaution, but it is hard to accept this view. After he or his staff have fixed a meeting, the same old story recurs: the person or group for whom the meeting has been arranged is asked to stay in the hotel and wait for a phone call. This is how it was in Beirut, in Tunis, and to a large extent still is in Gaza. People have waited and waited until the call finally comes, usually at an unreasonable hour somewhere around midnight. Now begins a dramatic series of events, with mysterious voices telling the people to present themselves within a few minutes at the entrance to the hotel. Here a car turns up (often late), they are collected by anonymous escorts, and taken with all speed to a meeting which in turn can often be delayed time and again.

Nearly all the journalists who have met Arafat have gone through this strange experience. One of them, Morgan Strong, first made an appointment with him in Beirut in 1982, but the meeting was canceled because of the war. Afterward, he followed

Arafat's footsteps for many weeks to Tunis, Amsterdam, Tunis again, Paris and Baghdad, where he finally completed the interview. In every place there was a repeat performance of the ritual, with the near-midnight phone call, the car which arrived late, and finally the meeting along with a night meal.

A Palestinian by the name of Dr. Afnan al-Qassen has told how he waited almost a month and a half for a meeting which had been arranged for him with Arafat in Tunis. When it never materialized, he gave up, left Tunis and wrote a book called *Waiting Forty Days for the President,*[113] describing his experience cooling his heels in the hotel and contending with PLO officials.

"On Sunday they told me 'Stay in your room, you'll get a call at night.' I was extremely happy and didn't sleep, but nothing happened. In the morning I was so worried and exasperated that I almost had a nervous breakdown. I called again and again until I got one of the officials on the phone and told him that after all Arafat had asked to see me, that they had sent me the plane tickets and that the PLO was paying the hotel bill. . . . I sat like a statue and waited while another day went by. My hotel room became a prison cell. In the evening I managed to get hold of Abu Marwan (Hakem Belawi, one of Arafat's assistants) and he shouted at me that the Commander wasn't there at all, he'd gone to Morocco and I should wait until he returned. I was told that I'd get a call tomorrow evening. I asked at what time and they replied that the evening was long—and cut me off. Once again I waited, not daring to move. I was sick and tired of the hotel food."

Dr. al-Qassen goes on to recount how he spent the next ten days in the hotel, in the streets of Tunis and in the waiting rooms of the PLO leaders, who looked as effective as trussed-up chickens. Finally, humiliated by the futility of being forever sent from one official to another, he wrote his book as an indictment of the Palestinian leadership. He saw these leaders as a corrupt body whose activities would cause grave harm to Palestinian culture and national interests.

Sarcastic and embittered, the book was dedicated to Arafat, and through its publication Dr. al-Qassen finally succeeded in getting attention from the PLO. In the course of 1993 several dozen copies arrived in East Jerusalem bookshops. One of the shop owners said that after he had sold a few copies, two young men arrived from the Fatah organization in the city and bought the whole remaining stock for the full price, so as to prevent its distribution.[114]

Similarly, Jerome Monod, president of a French economic corporation, described what happened to him in November of 1994 when he was to receive Arafat's confirmation for implementing development plans in the Gaza area. "I was compelled to wait 15 hours, after which they took me at 150 kilometers per hour through the streets of Tunis in order to meet a sick and dazed character who enfolded me in his arms and kissed me on my mouth." Following the publication of these words in the French press, the Palestinian Authority informed M. Monod of the cancellation of the contract, which was worth 5.7 million dollars.[115]

The confusion around Arafat's schedule has come to characterize all the working habits of the Palestinian leadership over which he presides. In the course of meetings in his office it is usual for him to deal simultaneously with a wide range of subjects, perpetually answering the phones, reading notes passed on to him by assistants, perusing files and documents, signing checks, and of course participating all the while in the discussion going on at the time.

Just as we have described him behaving courteously and relating personally to his guests, so has he also shown an ability to insult and hurt people and even to curse them in crude language. Rather than being mere outbursts, this behavior, I am convinced, is deliberate strategy. For example, in meetings of the PLO Executive Arafat has generally been very careful about directly attacking George Habash or Nayef Hawatmeh, the leftist opposition leaders. However, he has constantly insulted and humiliated Taysir Khaled, the representative of their organizations. Arafat does not create the sort of fearful atmosphere around him that would prevent people from directing criticism at him. But he has shown a great capacity for punishing and shunning people, and even for treading his critics underfoot.

During the whole year of 1993 he concealed from the Palestinian delegation to the Madrid Conference the existence of the other talks—the secret negotiations in Oslo. When they found out about this they undertook a sort of rebellion against him. In this instance, too, he refrained from abusing the chairperson of the delegation, Dr. Haidar Abdel Shafi, who had attacked Arafat in public. Not only is Dr. Abdel Shafi older than Arafat but he is also respected as a veteran Palestinian fighter. Arafat attacked younger members of the delegation instead.

For instance, Arafat once heard delegation member Saeb Erakat say during a television interview that he was thinking about resigning from his work in the Palestinian leadership and that he had plans to sit and write his memoirs. In the presence of dozens of people from the PLO leadership convened in Amman, Arafat turned to the younger man and asked him scornfully: "How long will it take you to write your memoirs, five minutes? And what will you do afterwards?"

Hanan Ashrawi is another junior associate he publicly humiliated in spite of her outstanding role in representing the Palestinians at the Madrid conference. When he found out that she had reservations about his methods of work, he reprimanded her in the presence of other people and said flatly: "I appointed you on the phone and I can fire you on the phone."

Some of Arafat's associates think that even his paroxysms of rage are premeditated. A political activist from Gaza participating for the first time as a guest in a meeting of the PLO Executive in Gaza was alarmed by Arafat's reaction to a speech by a representative of Nayef Hawatmeh's opposition organization. Arafat's whole body shook, the muscles of his neck swelled and his face turned red. It appeared to the guest that he was on the verge of a nervous breakdown or a heart attack, and he nervously pointed this out to his neighbors. They dismissed his fears, explaining that they had seen this on dozens of occasions and it was all an act—indeed, Arafat is a fine actor, completely in control of his whole body as well as his words.

Salah Khalaf (Abu Iyad) witnessed a comparable performance by Arafat during a conference with Arab leaders. At one of the meetings with Lebanese President Suleiman Franjieh Arafat interrupted the discussion: "Tears welled up in his eyes, he closed his notebook angrily . . . and exclaimed vehemently: 'I won't tolerate being spoken to in this way. I am a fighter! And it was because of my standing as a fighter that I was chosen to lead the Palestinian people, and not to win a majority of the votes in some meeting of dignitaries.' "[116]

In a visit to Libya at the end of 1977 a quarrel broke out between Arafat and Libyan Prime Minister Abdel Salam Jalloud in which Arafat raged against the Libyan with shouts and curses, finally leaving the official guesthouse in fury and slamming the door behind him. His hosts tried to stop him but he leaped into his car and departed at high speed. They searched for him for three hours and finally found him near the border with Tunis, where they persuaded him to return.[117]

Some of his outbursts are even more theatrical and he seems to enjoy staging dramatic episodes. As a twenty-three-year-old student leader he presented a petition to Egyptian President Mohammed Naguib (Nasser's predecessor) saying "Don't forget Palestine,"—written in blood. And in 1993 at the signing in Cairo of the peace treaty with Israel he was still mindful of the dramatic moment. There in the eyes of the whole world, Arafat disrupted the entire course of the ceremonial event by refusing to sign part of the documents.

Nabil Sha'ath, who has been Arafat's closest assistant since the signing of the peace agreement with Israel, says that to him, Arafat's behavior has sometimes seemed strange, and even exasperating and worrying.[118] The Chairman has had fits of anger, interrupting others or preventing them from speaking, and insisting that the last word be his. Others tell of diametrically opposite behavior and of how they have seen him begging for help and actually bursting into tears. The Israeli representatives who conducted negotiations with him have said that he has no hesitation in presenting himself as a pitiful wretch. His countenance would become miserable, his whole appearance would exude terrible depression and he would come out with pleas like "I'm sinking, I'm finished, you have to help me." Israeli Housing Minister Benyamin Ben-Eliezer, who visited Arafat in Tunis after the signing of the Declaration of Principles, hinted in the Israeli press that he saw the PLO leader actually weeping.

Many observers have been convinced that these are deliberate performances put on for the purpose of winning what he wants. In one meeting with representatives of Palestinians recently released from Israeli jails, the ex-prisoners asked to raise a series of petitions.[119] A spokesperson who had prepared the list in writing on their behalf started to read it. Arafat stopped him angrily and said: "Who are you to make demands of me?" They drew back, thinking that Arafat intended to rebuke them, and he continued in the same angry tone: "You must not ask a thing of me! You have just to give me orders. I am only here because you struggled and sat in prison and it is you who have to give me orders as to what to do." Arafat then instructed his assistants: "Listen to what these men have to say and carry out everything." He continued to praise and glorify the contribution of the prisoners to the Palestinian struggle and to declare his deep commitment to them. But the members of the delegation were given no opportunity to present their demands, and the meeting ended without any practical results.

All the Fatah activists have experienced these tricks but their efforts to overcome his machinations and inconsistency have been ineffectual. Arafat has brought people closer with one hand while rejecting them with the other. After making somebody wait for hours and humiliating him, he may hug and praise him, and then appoint him to a senior position. His associates find it hard to foresee his behavior and complain that he is so unpredictable they are in a state of permanent tension as to his reactions. On the other hand they have realized in working with him that this is one of his methods of safeguarding his power and authority.

All publications about the work of his office make note of the highly centralized character of Arafat's rule. Visitors compare it to a Byzantine court.[120] He has granted almost no authority to the people around him and makes all decisions alone. Arafat has an excellent memory. It is routine for him to go over nearly all the documents pertaining to his organization (and now to the Palestinian Authority which has been set up in Gaza) personally, creating extraordinary dependence upon him in every area. One member of the Authority says that each time he and his associates have approached Arafat with a request, he has asked them to stay and discuss it with him after the meeting. Thus all during the meeting they would sit on edge, reluctant to object to anything Arafat was saying because they were waiting to present their own request.

Arafat has always held sway in the Palestinian national movement and in the National Authority in the territories through personal rule. He has taken care to keep control over all information which reaches the various Palestinian institutions. Everyone must report to him in full detail while he himself provides his people only with partial and selective information. Whenever anyone opposes any of his ideas or proposals, Arafat whips out some piece of data unknown to his disputant. In the opinion of his assistants, the data might frequently be distorted, but nobody ever dares to disagree with him since he has made sure of being the only one with complete information.

Arafat has exploited the media to this end, too. He receives full and regular reports on the various publications relating to Middle Eastern politics. Large panels prepare up-to-date summaries for him of all press reports and radio and television broadcasts pertaining to the region, so Arafat has always been well-versed in hour-by-hour events in the Arab states, in Israel and of course in the Palestinian communities. One of his acquaintances once described him as "an addict of the media and the press." Among the notes given to him in his office during meetings, a considerable number are media reports on regional events. And for his own publicity, Arafat has always been accompanied by a permanent photographer as well as by bodyguards.

This sort of leadership structure is not really exceptional. There are many politicians who operate in a similar fashion, concentrating information in their own hands, dealing manipulatively with other people, refusing to delegate authority, accumulating power through pressure, guile, pretense, humiliation and intimidation of competitors and their backers, and exploiting the mass media through intrigues. Arafat's outstanding quality has been his success in safeguarding his leadership for so many years in spite of being without either territory or any coercive apparatus. On the surface, his Fatah movement, and the Palestinian movement as a whole, do have properly regulated institutions—councils, committees, bureaucracies. However, Arafat's control over all these has been almost total and he has succeeded in maneuvering so that the various institutions almost invariably adopt decisions which he supports. The Palestinian Authority which was established in Gaza operates along the same lines, all its offices and authorities managed in effect under Arafat's sole leadership.

If part of the secret of Arafat's control over his people is information management, the real key is in his complete supervision over the financial structure of the movement. Since the early 1970s the PLO has not been a poor organization. One of his assistants once said: "We are not a revolution of hungry people, but of people who understand that even if there is sufficient food, it is not enough." On the other hand Israeli spokespeople have more than once described the PLO as the richest national movement in human history. Monies transmitted to the PLO since Arafat consolidated his leadership have, indeed, been estimated in the billions of dollars. Since the PLO (and the various political organizations within it) never publishes its budget, no exact record of the figures is available. Its institutions and apparatus, both civilian and military, have behaved during all these years as an underground movement, keeping most of their activity secret, including the subject of finances.

Arafat has maintained sole control over financial affairs and he has been quoted as saying that "only he who controls the money maintains power."[121] Moreover, all PLO activists have borne witness that PLO bank accounts and financial assets are registered in Arafat's name. In other words, Arafat has made no distinction between private accounts and those of the movement. He has personally signed all checks going from his office to all the departments and activities of the organization, and banks are instructed to honor only checks with his signature. Each departmental director is given separate checks for every item: the secretary's wages, flight tickets, telephone bills, hotels, car, and so on. Every month he would sign hundreds or even thousands of checks, and all PLO officials were entirely dependent upon him for their expenses. Even with the establishment of the Palestinian Authority in Gaza he has generally continued this same system.

This manner of dealing with financial matters is one of the subjects which has served his opponents. For example Moustafa Tlass, who was Syrian Defense Minister, once said that Arafat has an absolute obsession with financial affairs and that judging from bank accounts registered in his name he is one of the richest men on earth.[122] He has pointed out that Arafat always demands that money transferred to the PLO from Arab countries be in his private name. Tlass has also brought up examples of the anarchy and corruption with which Arafat is said to deal with money. For example, he received ten ambulances from Kuwait during the Lebanon war and at once sold them at half-price to the Syrians. On another occasion Arafat tried to bribe Tlass with a BMW car as a gift. After some time Tlass found that the car had originally been stolen from the American Embassy in Amman, and he returned it to its owners.

Arafat has claimed in interviews that during his years in Kuwait (1957–1964) he accumulated a great deal of money and even became a millionaire. This is doubtful. It is clear, however, that at the beginning of his political activity he and his comrades contributed from their own money to Fatah and the PLO's expenses. And when they embarked on their first military action against Israel they had an overdraft of some hundreds of dollars on their bank account.[123] It was only in 1965 that they succeeded in getting some moderate contributions from donors in the Gulf principalities and in Lebanon (as well as assistance in arms and training from Algeria). Almost immediately, in 1966, there occurred the first financial scandal in the organization.

This was in all probability the only occasion when Yasser Arafat was dismissed from his position in the organization. One of his biographies quotes the resolution of Fatah's Central Committee dismissing Arafat "because of irresponsible expenditure, failure to implement collective decisions and presenting false reports primarily on military matters."[124] In the end this resolution was not implemented, but it is interesting that even then the negative aspects of Arafat's work were noticed: arbitrariness in expenditure, the striving for personal rule and a lack of credibility.

In the thirty years since then, the leopard has not changed his spots. As the Palestinian movement gained momentum, giant sums of money began to flow into the Fatah treasury, and later into the PLO treasury. Most came from taxes which the Arab states (principally the oil states) levied upon Palestinians working within their borders. Other contributions and assistance reached the PLO from additional countries, mainly East European. The peak was reached following the signing of the peace treaty between Egypt and Israel when a conference was convened in Baghdad aimed at blocking the possibility of other Arab nations siding with Egyptian policy. For this purpose massive sums were allocated to the PLO and to Jordan. (1979)

A considerable part of this money was used for the establishment of Palestinian health, educational, and welfare services in the occupied territories and elsewhere. Much money was also invested in the building up of PLO military units in Lebanon and in deploying a network of over a hundred embassies straddling the whole world. Rumor has it that Arafat gave orders as well to invest large sums of money in the purchase of assets in various parts of the world. PLO activists then behaved with an eye-boggling extravagance which aroused criticism among opponents and friends alike.

It would be difficult to say how many people apart from Arafat know full details of the secret accounts in banks all over the world. They perhaps number two or three, and even that is not certain. On the night when Arafat's plane crashed in the Libyan desert in April 1992, after emerging wounded and bruised from the aircraft, he helped tend to others who had been injured. However, he was no less concerned about finding the secret suitcase which he always carries with him. In it was a notebook containing details of the bank accounts. He searched in the wreckage of the plane, climbing up and down the surrounding sand dunes. One of his assistants said that had Arafat been killed or the notebook burned, nobody would have had any idea where to look for the money.[125] The suitcase was finally found.

In the period following the Gulf War, the PLO's financial situation deteriorated. Saudia Arabia and the Gulf states stopped transferring money to the Palestinian movement. In addition, the regimes in Eastern Europe which had assisted the PLO no longer existed. A considerable part of the network of services which the PLO had established collapsed. Budgetary cuts were introduced in the various offices and many of the activists and soldiers ceased receiving wages. But the arrangement according to which Arafat himself signed the checks continued as usual.

In those days delegations of Israeli Arabs often made visits to Tunis and held meetings with Arafat. During one of these, Salem Jubran, a journalist from Nazareth, saw Arafat routinely signing a check during the conversation. Arafat showed him that it was for the sum of several thousand dollars, intended for urgent medical treatment in Europe for the daughter of one of the activists. Jubran exclaimed: "You, the President of Palestine, have to deal with this? It's a matter for one of the organization's officials." But Arafat shook his head in disagreement and said: "No, only me."

riddle and solution

What does this accumulation of detail, this odd body of facts, lies, strategies and tricks, add up to? Can we now propose a solution to the riddle of Yasser Arafat? What has emerged is how accurately and persistently he has reflected the distress and the needs of the Palestinian public in a period when they were suffering from the humiliating defeat of the 1948 war. This is the key to his success. A number of characteristics which are part and parcel of Arafat's personality transformed him into a myth, and pushed into the background those other aspects of his personality which were repellent and ridiculous.

The loss of home and land, of respect and identity, were conceived by the Palestinians in the 1950s as an intolerable humiliation. Driven out of "the lost Paradise," as the Palestinian historian Araf al-Araf put it, they were scattered to the four winds. A small minority remained in the state of Israel where a military government was forced upon them and their rights as citizens restricted. The rest were subjected to the rule of the neighboring Arab states: Jordan ruled the West Bank and Egypt the Gaza Strip, while hundreds of thousands were housed in temporary camps in Lebanon and Syria.

The pain of losing mastery over the homeland grew sharper when in 1967 Israel conquered the West Bank and Gaza and transformed the Palestinian residents there into subjects of an alien and oppressive military rule. The suffering made all parts of the dispersed Palestinian population into partners on one definitive issue, with a common and concrete goal—to return home. This meant not literally the simple return to a house in Haifa or to an orange grove in Jaffa, but a return to living as rulers of their own fate: to put an end to being "people of nowhere," and to become again masters of their own place. A place on the map, a place in history.

Many of them felt that they had been transformed "from being a person to being a situation." Instead of an individual with a name and a status, each had become a vague and general concept, a "problem" rather than a human being. Instead of Abu Daoud from the village of Mansoura in Galilee or Abu Ahmed from Breir in the South, this man without a homeland became a problematic "refugee" in Gaza, or a worrisome "Palestinian" in Lebanon, or "a local resident" obstructing the Israeli authorities in the West Bank. It was as if their individual identities had been wiped out. "Go and buy something in the Palestinian's store," parents would tell children in Damascus, in Kuwait or in Beirut—just "a Palestinian" without a name or face. As they saw it, the Palestinian distress, or "problem," did not evoke an adequate echo or gain its deserved recognition in the eyes of those around them. It was in need of a representative symbol.

Yasser Arafat provided all this with considerable success. "The PLO is our homeland, and Abu Ammar is our identity," was a well-known saying in the concentrations of Palestinians in the 1970s and 1980s. The question of how Arafat did this, what means he used, was not particularly important or relevant. Arafat's hyperbole and fabrications were not taken into consideration as long as they served the cause effectively. The use of terrorism, the theatrics, and the absurd imagery were mainly in the eyes of outside observers, of foreign leaders and of hostile public opinion in Western countries and in Israel. The Palestinian population, and to some extent also the masses in the Arab countries, were won over by the new myth of his image.

When relating to the past, Arafat sketches the mythology of Palestinian suffering, the suffering of the oppressed, in sharp lines. "Did you know that even Spartacus was a Palestinian?" Arafat once said to a journalist who was interviewing him. He apparently meant by this to suggest a historical continuity between slaves revolting against Rome two thousand years ago and the Palestinians revolting against the Israelis in the occupied territories. Arafat has also called Jesus Christ, another famous victim, the "Palestinian Messiah."[126]

As the hero of Palestinian national mythology, Arafat enjoyed great freedom in interpreting both past and present events. The Palestinian past was one of struggle against that alien and domineering Zionist force which had driven the Palestinians from their homeland. This was the purpose of those exaggerations and misconstructions with which Arafat painted a conceptual picture of the enemy in Palestinian eyes. This was Zionist Israel on whose Parliament building there must naturally be the map projecting Israeli conquests from the Nile in Egypt to the Euphrates in Iraq. A map like this must of course be found in the Knesset, and not only according to Palestinian beliefs. The whole Arab world is convinced that this is not fabriction, but a firm fact.

And against the evil Zionism with its expansionist ambitions, Arafat would present the ideal of the anti-Zionist religious Jew. Such is Rabbi Moshe Hirsch of the ultra-orthodox Neturei Karta, who was to be a brother and partner in the vision of the democratic Palestinian state where people of all religions would live in equality and harmony. In the Israeli reality Rabbi Moshe Hirsch is a farce, a figure of fun. In the Palestinian and general Arab-Muslim reality on the other hand, Rabbi Hirsch was the epitome of the ideal Jew. With him and his kind one could live in peace because, lacking any national political ambitions, he is ready to be satisfied even with the rights of a tolerated religious minority in an Arab state.

When Arafat invited him, symbolically of course, to be a minister in the Palestinian government which was being established in Gaza, it was seen in Israel as yet another idiotic joke on the part of a leader who was not to be taken seriously. But the Palestinians did not so much as raise their eyebrows in surprise. Arafat even hung Rabbi Hirsch's oath of loyalty on the wall of his office in Gaza. Not a single Palestinian had anything to say against this and no one asked him to put an end to this odd friendship with such an outlandish character.

These two examples, with which we began our inquiry, the Knesset "map" and Rabbi Moshe Hirsch, are indeed characteristic of Arafat's behavior. As always, he is trying to provide the Palestinian revolution, of which he is the center, with legitimacy. To Arafat and to the Palestinian public these examples demonstrate who is the enemy and why he must be fought against, and who is the friend and partner.

Arafat's image as a Palestinian national myth has had a clear purpose. It was fostered by him and by his environment as a focus of mobilization for political activity. A myth is not necessarily a lie. It is built on a factual basis which is then adapted, expanded and consolidated. Yasser Arafat's biography, his characteristics as an individual and his actual deeds, have been exploited for the national Palestinian cause. His being a bachelor for years, his appearance, his energy, his military past, his wanderings as one who is homeless, his almost miraculous survival, his simple lifestyle— in all these there is a foundation of truth which was reshaped in order to serve the myth of Mr. Palestine, embodying the image of the Palestinian problem in his person.

The first to believe in the myth which was thus created was Arafat himself, along with the founders of the Fatah organization. They believed that they were the victims of the whole world around them, of their enemies—above all of Israel and the West—

and also of the Arab regimes which betrayed them. Their deep belief in the justice of their cause created a sense of moral superiority within their ranks.

The Palestinian revolution, which Arafat represented, looked in their eyes so pure and unsullied that it was entitled to contend even with the moral strength of the Jewish state which had arisen after the Holocaust of European Jewry. Concerning the Lebanese war, Arafat said to his sympathetic biographer, Allan Hart: "It is not really my way to compare the Israelis or some Israelis with the Nazis. I don't think it really serves any purpose to speak in such a way.... But I have to tell you something from deep inside me. When I think over ... the firepower the Israelis have used to try and liquidate my poorly armed and mainly unarmed refugee people, a people with justice on their side, I think it is fair to say that Israelis, some Israelis, have behaved like Nazis."[127]

According to this formula, Arafat could preach to Jews that the occupation and rule over another people was contrary to Jewish tradition, history, and morality. "Now we are the victims," Arafat was to repeat time and time again as he described the death of children, infants, and mothers in the days of the Intifada.[128]

The myth of the victim and of moral superiority was fostered by Arafat and his people in order to create guilt feelings in the Arab world. Referring to the Palestinians, he has more than once[129] declared "I am the conscience of the Arab nation." And as such he is the epitome of purity, not putting his trust in, nor needing, the Arab rulers. Arafat is certain that the Arab masses support him, recognizing that his is a just cause.[130]

It has often happened that Arafat and his people became prisoners of the myth of their moral superiority to the extent that they erred in evaluating their own strength and made mistakes which cost them dearly. In 1970 in Jordan, Arafat was certain that King Hussein would not dare to go to war against the PLO as representative of Palestinian justice. The Palestinian leadership was convinced that the Arab masses in Jordan and elsewhere would prevent a war aimed at expelling the PLO from the Kingdom of Jordan and that Jordanian soldiers would not obey orders to destroy the Palestinian presence. Because of this incorrect evaluation, the Palestinian movement suffered a tough military defeat. Thousands of Palestinians were killed, the infrastructure of the Palestinian movement in Jordan was destroyed and Arafat was compelled to start afresh in Lebanon.

Arafat was also certain that as "the conscience of the Arab nation" he could prevent President Sadat from signing the peace agreement with Israel. Here too he failed. Fifteen years later, in the 1993 Oslo agreements, Arafat accepted a plan for partial Palestinian autonomy in the territories which was far more limited than the autonomy he could have acquired according to the Israeli-Egyptian agreements signed in Camp David in 1978.

Arafat was excused for such mistakes just as dozens of falsifications in announcements on so-called victories against the Israeli enemy in the period before and after the 1967 war were forgotten. After all, he symbolized the just Palestinian cause which was bound, as it were, to triumph against a helpless and defeated Arab world. According to Arafat, the Palestinians served for decades as the doormat on which the Arab states trod. As a youth he personally had been forced to collect antique weapons in the desert for the 1948 war because the Arab armies wouldn't arm the Palestinians. Subsequently, they disarmed him (and the Palestinians in general) and refused to permit them to fight for the salvation of their own homeland.

Therefore, when he and his comrades announced the launching of "the armed struggle," they were not concerned with making truthful reports of what occurred in their military actions. In the eyes of Arafat and his colleagues, it was the actual Palestinian readiness to go to war which was of prime importance—the breakthrough itself and the precedent it created. This strain of nationalistic romanticism bestowed upon the PLO's military activity,

under Arafat's command, a dimension of heroism which confounded factual observation of the scene. The way the PLO
fighters posed before the television cameras, the marches, the
songs and the flags, as well as the military announcements, were
of tremendous value to Arafat and the Palestinians.

In retrospect it appears that he was right. The Arafat myth won
amazing success. The leader and "the problem" achieved powerful
international support. Under Arafat's leadership, the PLO gained
the recognition of 120 states in all parts of the the world, an un-
precedented success for a national movement lacking a territory.
Of course it was assisted by the political circumstances in which
it functioned. Eretz Yisrael/Palestine, the Holy Land, which was
the goal of his movement, was and remains a focus of international interest for hundreds of millions of believers. Arafat conducted his struggle against the Jewish state on the broad field of
the Middle East as an international strategic crossroad, and as the
largest concentration of oil reserves in the world, with the widespread guilt feelings over the horrors of the Second World War
hovering in the background.

The success that Arafat and the Palestinian movement experienced in penetrating public consciousness in Europe and America
was also due to the social and ideological crises which overtook
the West in the late 1960s and through the 1970s. Students and
young people declared war on the bourgeois and conservative
establishments of their countries. Violent clashes with students in
France spread to all of West and Central Europe, urban underground movements were set up, such as the Red Brigades in Italy,
the Baader-Meinhof group in Germany, and militant student and
black groups in the United States, where protest against the Vietnam War became a central theme for the New Left.

In this climate, Arafat's symbolic image was received with
great sympathy, confirming leftist accusations that the Western
democratic establishment which supported Israel was insincere

and hypocritical. He became the "noble savage," the sacrificial native victim exploited and enslaved by the corrupt economic interests of the Western powers.

Arafat's struggle also served to tranquilize Western guilt over the Holocaust. Here the ancient roles of David and Goliath seemed to be reversed, with the Arab Palestinians becoming the oppressed people fighting for freedom against a strong and well-equipped Jewish army. Arafat would say, "the Jews are indeed victims, and we the Palestinians are the victims of the victims." In the Western democracies, this new perception also allowed latent anti-Semitic instincts to emerge, strengthening tendencies to cleanse the guilt feelings from the Holocaust.

All these factors focused worldwide attention on the Middle East. Over the years the Palestinians, Israel, and the whole Middle Eastern conflict generated an usually wide range of media coverage. There were years, for example in the peak period of the Intifada, when for months on end photos of events in the West Bank and Gaza never left the world's television screens. Dr. Meron Benvenisti, an Israeli reseacher into the conflict, once said that in order to raise an echo as strong as their distress, it was not enough for the Palestinians to have good drumsticks. They also needed a drum good enough to provide powerful resonance. The Holy Land constituted this sort of drum. Are there not wars and local conflicts—tribal, ethnic and national—in a whole series of distant parts of the world like Africa and central Asia, where the atrocities which take place often fail to reverberate in the media? What would have happened, for example, if the Palestinians had been subject to Turkish oppression in eastern Anatolia? Who would have heard about them?

If one asks to what extent political circumstances caused Arafat to become the standard-bearer of the Palestinian myth, this is the sort of historiographical question to which there is no answer. The emphasis must be on an evaluation of the political intuition of Arafat as a person, and his understanding of how "to transform the Palestinians from objects of history, whose history is made without them and by others, into the subjects of history, in the making of which they participate."[131] Though many observers see him as a repellent character, lacking credibility, often grotesque, Arafat became a source of inspiration to his own people, a leader who, unlike many modern leaders, is not led by his people but leads them.

And he has led the Palestinians along a well-defined course whose end could be foreseen from its beginning. The emphasis which Arafat put from the start on Palestinian national identity as existing in its own right and as superior to other components of identity, to a large degree determined the creation of a new reality in the Middle East. Definitions of self-identity like Arab, Muslim, Socialist, or those subscribing to some other ideology—these were pushed aside from the beginning by Arafat in favor of the definition "Palestinian."

Thus his keen political sense led him to understand that a contradiction exists between the fostering of this identity and the aspiration to gain control over the whole of Palestine. In other words, Arafat understood that a price must be paid for placing so much emphasis upon Palestinian particularism: the more the Palestinians emphasize their existence as an entity separate from other Arab peoples, the more difficult it will be to overcome the state of Israel. The Palestinians are a relatively small and weak people. They will never succeed alone in struggling to replace Israel with a Palestinian state in the whole territory of the country.

"I did indeed dream of the establishment of a democratic state in the whole area of Palestine," said Arafat in 1983 "but I know that this is a difficult objective. Even establishing a Palestinian state according to the 1947 partition borders may not be possible, but the establishment of a Palestinian state in the area of the West Bank and Gaza is certainly possible."[132] This is a realistic and pragmatic ambition compared with what might look possible to those who placed the concept of membership in the great Arab nation as a whole above particular Palestinian identity. In that way one could indeed believe in the possibility of establishing a "greater Palestine." But only a nonexistent unity and cooperation throughout the Arab world could mobilize the resources necessary for a struggle which would defeat and overthrow the state of Israel.

So it happened that Arafat brought about a dramatic change in the Palestinian position toward the state of Israel, moving in a direction which, if one now looks back, was apparent almost from the very beginning. Through complex and tortuous political maneuvering, Arafat succeeded in altering the course of the Palestinian national movement. From a "total position" demanding acquisition of the whole territory and elimination of the state of Israel, it moved to a "relative position" of readiness to compromise on the West Bank and the Gaza Strip, which make up only about a quarter of the area of the country. On the strength of his great prestige as the father of the renaissance of the Palestinian people, he gradually shifted the Palestinian demands from the heights of inflexible and uncompromising ideology, to the pragmatic and feasible ground of the existing reality.

Arafat was successful in this historic achievement because of his ability to unite and rally his people around those symbols of legitimacy which they had desperately needed in the particular historical circumstances within which they were operating. He was the product of the pain and humiliation to which they were subject and he expressed this in all the component parts of his personality, harsh and absurd as these may be.

His personality is therefore not so enigmatic and mysterious as it may at first appear. It is true that it involves the use of rhetorical clichés, distortions, and cunning trickery. But all this comes to serve the lofty aim of mobilizing the Palestinian people. They, and in their wake the Arab states, the whole world, and even the government of Israel were persuaded that Arafat was the Palestinian problem and accordingly he and only he could solve it.

fading magic, fading myth

In the summer of 1994 Arafat began establishing the first Palestinian self-rule in the homeland. This was a highly significant turning point for him and for the Palestinian movement embodied by the PLO. Here was no longer a national movement in exile seeking recognition of its status, but an administration trying to mold the first Palestinian authority in its own land. In view of the high expectations there is, however, some doubt as to whether Arafat's first steps on Palestinian soil can be called a great success. Following a few first weeks of euphoria after taking over Gaza and Jericho, it looked as if Arafat was quickly forfeiting his status and prestige among the Palestinians, until people even began to ask whether his time was up.

The main problems of the Palestinian Authority, the temporary government which was established in Gaza and in Jericho, stemmed from the character of the agreements which Arafat had signed with Israel. These gave him only a limited autonomous authority over a small area of the country. He was opposed not only by those negating the whole peace process, like the Islamic groups and the "rejectionist" organizations centered in Damascus, but also by many of his traditional supporters. Some of these saw the agreements as a "surrender move" which made Arafat into a collaborator who was implementing the continuation of Israeli rule. Others refused to accept the perpetuation of his style of leadership.

Even his veteran associates have turned their backs on him. On 15 November 1994, the sixth anniversary of the Palestinian Declaration of Independence (proclaimed by the Palestinian National Council in Algiers in 1988), Arafat planned the first ceremonial meeting of the PLO Executive on the soil of the homeland, in Gaza. Less than half the members arrived (eight out of eighteen) so that in effect the meeting had no legal validity.

Farouk Kaddoumi, the only one left of the five Fatah founders, completely boycotted the peace moves. Mahmoud Abbas (Abu Mazen), also one of the few left from the early leadership, though he supported Arafat and stood by him when the agreements were signed, adamantly refused to work with him in the Authority set up in Gaza. Though not in public, he has said that he is no longer able to stomach Arafat's leadership methods. Prominent personalities representing broad Palestinian circles, like the poet Mahmoud Darwish, Haidar Abdel Shafi, Abdullah Hourani and others, would not cooperate with Arafat. The leadership of the "People's Party" (formerly communist), which had been a faithful partner of Arafat in the whole peace process, broke off contact with him. Some of the groups and persons refused not out of principled opposition to the agreements, but because they realized that Arafat had not changed his style of leadership.

Everything has remained the same: Arafat's one-man rule, the manipulation of people and groups associated with him, the work patterns. In his Gaza office, which is copied almost exactly from Tunis, the endless meetings of those close to him have continued, without regular institutions being installed. Arafat works personally on all administrative subjects of Palestinian rule and involves himself in all offices of the Authority. There are complaints of colossal inefficiency. The Gazans say, "He appoints at least three drivers for the same car and demands they all drive at the same time." In Tunis the Fatah and PLO committees and councils lacked clear status and underwent haphazard changes in accordance with the Chairman's whims. In Gaza, too, the machinery of the National Authority is an almost random collection of people appointed by Arafat. He promotes, ignores or dismisses people at will and this is how all appointments have been made. None of the appointees is ever tested for their qualifications or examined by any objective body.

The decisions of the Palestinian Authority have continued to be made casually, as in the PLO, in accordance with Arafat's capricious policy, which in many cases is not clear to anyone. He has neither delegated authority nor begun the training of an appropiate leadership for the administration of affairs of state.[133]

His daily schedule remains frequently mysterious, as in the underground, and he still tends to disappear and make sudden journeys without announcing his plans. He has not, however, as many had forecast, continued his inveterate round of travel, staying in Gaza most of the time. But in other ways his administrative habits have not changed. Arafat has continued in the new Authority, as in the old PLO days, to see money as the source of power, signing checks alone and keeping the secrets of the budget to himself. Since his administration lacks financial resources, Arafat has been taking a significant commission from every business deal made between people from Gaza and foreigners. Thus, for example, building contractors from Gaza who buy cement from Israel through the offices of the Palestinian Authority have paid a twenty percent levy above the official price. In one meeting at the end of December 1994, the residents complained loudly about the prices of flour and sugar, claiming that Arafat took three dollars for every sack coming into Gaza by the Erez crossing with Israel. Arafat exploded angrily at them, shouting that he would go with them himself to the Erez crossing and prove that this charge was false.

Despite his constant meetings with entrepreneurs, engineers, bankers and economists, slow progress if any has been made. Money from the "contributing countries" which was supposed to bring economic prosperity to Gaza has long been delayed because Arafat found it difficult to set up the necessary machinery to assure that these monies would actually be directed to economic goals. Confronted with this procrastination at implementing World Bank instructions, he asked angrily "Who needs their money in any case? I have enough rich Palestinians who will bring billions to the country." But the first months of Palestinian rule in Gaza brought not economic prosperity but a frightening economic retreat. Time and again the crossings to Israel have been closed because of violent acts by Muslim extremists against Israelis. Tens of thousands of workers from Gaza who made their living in Israel have found themselves without work. At the beginning of the Palestinian autonomy in Gaza the unemployment rate was already estimated to be over fifty percent. Arafat promised illusory schemes for housing, industry, ports and airports, all for immediate execution within months. "We will implement the economic miracle of Singapore here," Arafat announced.

At a typical meeting near the end of 1994 with 200 dignitaries from the city of Gaza, Arafat listened to complaints about the collapse of the wretched road system and terrible problems with drainage, the electricity network, telephones, etc. They were not afraid to tell him that the conduct of his whole administration was a failure. But at the end of the meeting, they all stood in line to be photographed shaking hands with the Chairman and embracing him. Each of them later received his personal photograph taken with Arafat, like a sports hero or Hollywood star. This is one of his familiar ruses for eliciting sympathy.

Arafat's critics in Gaza have been first and foremost those who saw the agreement with Israel as a humiliating defeat. However, there are also others who at first believed that even if the agreement were a bad one, it at least holds out a possibility of continuing the struggle for independence. One of these, the psychiatrist Iyad Sharraj explains that while in former periods the Palestinians had conducted a stormy romance with Arafat, now the days of marriage, which by their nature kill romance, have come. In an open letter to Arafat he writes: "Soon the honeymoon will be over and now you, Arafat, must work hard and develop along with us real relations and build a true partnership."[134]

Like many other residents of the West Bank and Gaza, Sharraj was not prepared to accept the style of operation of the revolutionary who worked at night, whom it was so hard to reach, who doesn't maintain organized administrative institutions. In addition to poor work arrangements, stories have circulated of corruption in the Palestinian leadership and an inability to correct the irregularities.

Arafat has stuck adamantly to the elements which would preserve his leadership as embodying the myth of the Palestinian national entity, but to many it appears that there is no longer any need for this. Palestinian and foreign entrepreneurs considering investment in Gaza want to work with an orderly machinery and organized institutions. Instead of this they have found the old leadership, totally dependent upon the haphazard decisions of one individual.

In consequence, promised investments have not arrived. The Israeli authority left behind a ruined infrastructure, poverty and backwardness in Gaza. A different sort of leader was needed now in order to rehabilitate the ruins: not the theatrical figure of a restless politician, but an administrator who knows how to operate an efficient machinery. Not an unshaven man in military uniform, but an executive in a gray suit with a respectable appearance. The combination of a suspicious Israeli government, which has succeeded in pinning Arafat down to a complicated and restrictive agreement, and a Palestinian leadership inexperienced in management have given rise to fears for the future of the Palestinian Authority.

In Gaza, the Arafat magic increasingly began to melt away. The myth dissolved as it looked more and more superfluous. Now that as the symbol of their national struggle he has achieved legitimacy for the Palestinians, Arafat appears on the surface to have fulfilled his historical task. Without vision and myth the Palestinians could not have reached the point to which Arafat has brought them. However, one cannot govern by myth alone. Even before his arrival in Gaza, many sensed this, opponents and sympathizers alike. One of the reactions to Arafat's emerging alive when his plane crashed in the Libyan desert two years before was that though Arafat had survived, his time was almost up.[135]

His time was also up according to many of his acquaintances who looked fearfully at the attitude with which Arafat regarded democratic ways and human rights. Edward Said is not alone in fearing "a marriage between the chaos of civil war in Lebanon and the tyranny of Sadam Hussein's Iraq."[136] On the one hand Arafat demanded immediate elections and on the other he prevented attempts to promote democratic processes in his own government. The distribution of the newspaper *Al-Nahar* was prohibited at his orders because it expressed pro-Jordanian positions, and other Palestinian papers have been restricted.[137] At his instructions the process of internal elections for the branches of the Fatah organization in the West Bank was stopped, because his people were not succeeding there.

The organization of general elections in the territories also depends, according to the agreement, on cooperation with Israel, and Israel has been in no hurry to push them. Neither, however, could one see in Arafat's government any significant effort to prepare for these elections. In October 1994 Arafat declared that come what may, the elections would take place in November—that is, within four to five weeks, when nobody had yet done the necessary preparatory work. There was no prospect of implementing his declaration. Even without an agreement with Israel, the preparation of the electoral roll, the publicity campaigns of the different parties, the registration of the candidates and other technical arrangements would take many months. There were even Palestinians who claimed that the whole business of elections was designed, in Arafat's view, to find an arrangement which would ensure his election as life-President.

A further source of tension has been Arafat's cultivation of the old population of permanent residents in the West Bank and Gaza at the expense of refugee families. Although in Gaza refugees make up over 60 percent of the population, and in the West Bank about 30 percent, his appointments to city councils have been almost exclusively from the old, established families, whose large assets could promote his economic initiatives. Palestinian refugees abroad are also neglected now. While Arafat concentrates on building a power base among the permanent population on the West Bank, and according to the Oslo agreement a solution to the refugee problem is deferred to a later stage, Palestinian populations in Jordan, Syria, and Lebanon, as well as the veteran PLO leadership, have become increasingly bitter and frustrated.

But the fracturing of the Arafat myth in Gaza and the West Bank has been mainly the work of the fanatical Islamic groups. Perhaps for the first time since he won for himself the elevated title of Mr. Palestine, there have arisen significant organizations which forcefully challenge this status. It is true that in the past Arafat has overcome many attempts to dethrone him. These were generally cases of subversion supported by the intelligence services of Arab states, such as the revolt against him in 1983 of people from the Fatah machinery, with Syrian support. Arafat fought successfully for many years against various opposition organizations, led by the Popular Front (PFLP) and the Democratic Front (DFLP). Never, however, did he find himself forced to stand up against a relatively large body of his own people who refused to recognize him and what he stood for.

The Palestinian Islamic groups are not homogeneous. Their base is to be found in a broad stratum of conservative believers for whom the revolutionary fervor of Arafat and the PLO has never been acceptable. For many of them the revolutionary approach favored by the Palestinian national movement was even a sort of threat. The PLO slogans for a secular state, its contacts with the communist governments, and the strong presence of Marxist groups in the movement, dismayed the conservative circles among the Palestinians in the West Bank and Gaza.

Most of these middle-class town-dwellers, merchants, professionals and well-to-do villagers, strove to preserve the status quo. For many years they had been inclined to support orthodox Islamic organizations, including wings of the Muslim Brothers, participating in the activities of the Islamic establishment in their vicinity. According to the Islamic commandments, they collected donations for the organization of different categories of social work. Among other things they established schools, hostels for orphans, kindergartens, clinics for the needy, and welfare institutions. For an extended period the Israeli military government supported these groups, and this to some extent counterbalanced the PLO's militant nationalist activity.

In the mid-1980s there grew out of these orthodox groups an extremist movement influenced by the fanatical course of fundamentalist Islam, which was rising in the region following the success of the Khomeini revolution in Iran. This movement was called Hamas (initials for the Islamic Resistance Movement) and its people, along with smaller fanatical Islamic groups, began violent attacks upon Israelis. They were the harbingers of the national uprising, the Intifada, which was later to be sustained by the infrastructure of nationalist institutions which the PLO had established.[138]

Hamas refused to accept the definitions of national identity and national goals which Arafat had formulated. In the eyes of

Muslim zealots, belonging to the Palestinian people did not stand above everything else. Islam was for them more important and they believed the Palestinians should behave according to its precepts. The Hamas program accordingly rejected out of hand the PLO's political compromise with the state of Israel.

In the course of the 1980s and afterward, in the period of the Madrid conference (1991), Arafat employed a number of tactics designed to tame them and bring them into the framework of the national home, i.e. the PLO. He set up within the PLO a religious movement which would compete with them, offering the Hamas positions and budgets and conducting protracted discussions in order to persuade them. The ideological split between Hamas and Arafat was indeed considerable, but what completely destroyed any possibility of cooperation was their demand to receive forty percent of the positions in PLO institutions. This would mean Arafat's losing much of his ability to control his organization, and he furiously rejected the demand. In a meeting with Hamas representatives in Khartoum, the Sudanese capital, in 1992, he said that to accept their demands would mean that he would have to resign from his position as PLO Chairman.

This was one of the few occasions when Arafat has spoken of resigning. In his youth he had been fully acquainted with the Muslim Brothers movement and was himself to a certain extent connected with it. His first arrest in Cairo in 1954 was due to the Egyptian authorities' suspicion that he was active in an underground group of the Brothers. Deep down it appears that he is a believing Muslim. He was raised in a traditional and orthodox family and his spiritual world is that of Islam. His heroes are Islamic heroes and his speeches rich with quotes from verses of the Koran. Yet in spite of his observance of the religious commands, Arafat is accustomed to praying only once a day (instead of five times). "I concentrate all the prayers in one," Arafat has often said.[139]

Precisely because of this background Arafat has difficulty in contending with Muslim zealots from among his own people. When some of his opponents conjectured that there was a possibility that Arafat would be murdered by his enemies in Gaza, the reference was to an action by Muslim zealots.[140] At least one Muslim group, the Islamic Jihad led by Dr. Fathi Shkaki, announced early in 1994 that it is permissible to kill Arafat.

The Arafat myth is breaking up at the very time when he himself is back on Palestinian soil, at the height of his international prestige and as recipient of the Nobel Peace Prize, and with prospects on the horizon for achieving his dream of a Palestinian state. Now, however, the legend of Arafat seems of little use and appears to be disintegrating against the harsh background of Gaza. Each reality fosters or destroys its own myths. In this new reality, a solution is approaching to the mystery of Yasser Arafat's complex personality.

notes

FOREWORD

1. For instance the interview with Oriana Fallaci, *L'Europeo,* spring 1970.
2. The one which slanders him is *Arafat: the Man and the Myth* by Thomas Kiernan, W.W. Norton & Co. Inc., New York 1976. Those praising him are *Arafat: Terrorist or Peacemaker?* by Alan Hart, Sidgwick of Jackson, London, 1984; and *Arafat, A Key Personality* by Rashida Mahran, published in series form in Arabic in the paper *Al-Rai al-Am,* Kuwait, January 1987.

1: THE ENIGMA OF YASSER ARAFAT

3. *Ma'ariv* (Hebrew newspaper) Friday supplement, summer 1994 (on his arrival in Gaza). *On the question of terrorism:*

The term terrorism is subject to political, moral and other interpretations, and I have tried not to get involved in them. There is hardly a leader of a national movement in modern times who has not been called a terrorist by his opponents. Arafat likes to note that even George Washington was called a terrorist by the English. Along with this, there is no doubt that Arafat himself and his top people engaged in real terrorism in the years 1968 to 1974.

The great majority of the generally known Palestinian terrorist acts were carried out not by the Fatah organization under Arafat's leadership, but by the extreme Marxist organizations (PFLP and DFLP and other organizations) and later— and today—by fanatical Muslim organizations. The Fatah organization claimed to be acting against military installations and soldiers, but it was gradually dragged along behind the terrorist acts of the other organizations. After Karameh (March 1968) the position in Jordan deteriorated into a near civil war between the Palestinian organizations and the Jordanian army, and a crisis was reached in the summer of 1970 after the Marxist organizations hijacked civilian planes in Europe and flew them to Jordan. King Hussein attacked the Palestinians and drove them out following a series of battles in September of that year. Further battles ensued until the middle of 1971. As a result of the harsh defeat in Jordan, Arafat set up within Fatah a secret organization called Black September, whose people carried out a series of terrorist acts. These included the murder in Cairo of Jordanian Prime Minister Wasfi Tal and the attempted assassination of other Jordanian personalities. The best-known terrorist act was the murder of the Israeli athletes at the Munich Olympics in 1972.

As long as the only aim of Arafat (in Fatah and in the PLO) was to liberate the whole of Palestine and to destroy Israel (as described in the 1964 PLO Charter), in their eyes the use of terrorism was legitimate, though they did not use the word terror, but spoke of "armed struggle." After their defeat in Jordan (1970), the Palestinian groups, including Fatah, increased greatly their use of terror. They justified their actions by claiming that Israel was a terrorist state which bombed civilian targets (like Lebanese refugee camps) and whose very existence is founded on violation by force of Palestinian rights. Only after the October 1973 war and a range of political developments in 1974 did the PLO (under the leadership of Arafat and Fatah) become an organization also taking the political path. Arafat appeared in the United Nations and the PLO almost completely ceased terrorist actions abroad. Within the occupied territories, however, the Palestinian population was permitted to employ all methods in the struggle against the occupation, so that terrorism continued but in a different form.

4. For instance in the same *Playboy* interview, August 1988.

5. Nahum Barnea in the Hebrew newspaper *Yediot Ahronot,* 2 September 1994.

6. *From Beirut to Jerusalem,* an Anchor Book, Doubleday, 1989.

7. Translation from the Hebrew, in the newspaper *Hadashot,* 13 February 1992.

8. For instance in a working paper published by Yehoshafat Harkabi in Jerusalem, 6 March 1992; and Dr. Menaham Klein, who did research into internal relations within the PLO, in a conversation with the author, October 1994.

9. *Behind the Myth: Yasser Arafat and the Palestinian Revolution* by Andrew Gowers and Tony Walker, Corgi Books, Great Britain, 1990, pg 25. (Olive Branch Press issued an American edition in 1992.)

10. Alan Hart, see footnote 2, pg 36.

11. For instance in *Playboy*, see footnote 4.

12. Herbert Kelman, *Foreign Policy,* no. 49, Winter 1982/3.

13. Nahum Barnea, *Yediot Ahronot*, see footnote 5.

14. Gowers and Walker, see footnote 9, pg 472.

15. Edward W. Said, *The Progressive*, December 1993.

16. In an interview with Alexander Cockburn, *Los Angeles Times*, 20 October 1994.

2: CAIRO AND JERUSALEM

17. *Arafat: In the Eyes of the Beholder,* Janet and John Wallach, a Lyle Stuart Book, Carol Publishing Group, New York, 1990. Pg 15.

18. *Playboy*, see footnote 4.

19. Michal Sela, the Hebrew newspaper *Davar*, 1 July 1994.

20. Ehud Ya'ari, *Fatah* (Hebrew), A. Levin-Epstein, Tel Aviv, 1970, pg 10. (American edition in 1970 by Sabra Books, titled *Strike Terror: The Story of Fatah.*)

21. Wallach, see footnote 17, pgs 25–26.

22. Michal Sela, *Davar*, see footnote 19.

23. Wallach, see footnote 17, pg 26.

24. Interview in Amman to *Sawt al-Sha'ab,* 16 July 1983.

25. From research interviews conducted by Janet and John Wallach for their book (see footnote 17), which they were kind enough to place at my disposal.

26. Mahmoud Darwish, "The Identity of Absence," *Mifgash (Encounter)* 7–8, 1987.

27. The title of his Palestinian poems, *Victims of the Map*, Saqi Books, London, 1984.

28. Edward Said, *The Question of Palestine*, Vintage Books, New York, 1980.

29. "In The Crater of a Volcano," *Mifgash (Encounter)* 7–8, 1987.

30. A. L. Tibawi, "Visions of the Return," *Middle East Journal* 1963.

31. Fawaz Turki, *The Disinherited: Journal of a Palestinian Exile*, Monthly Review Press, New York, 1972.

32. Al-Sayyad Lebanon, from Ya'ari, see footnote 20, pg 133.

3: WHAT'S IN A NAME?

33. Interview in *Sawt al-Sha'ab* , Tunis, 14 July 1983.

34. Ya'ari, see footnote 20, pg 10.

35. Gowers and Walker, see footnote 9, pg 466.

36. Alan Hart, see footnote 2, pg 337.

37. "On the Road with Arafat" by T. D. Allman, *Vanity Fair*, February 1989.

38. For instance Uri Avneri, see footnote 3; or Nahum Barnea and Smadar Peri, *Yediot Ahronot*, 27 November 1992.

39. See footnote 2.

40. Dan Avidan, *Davar,* 9 November 1985.

41. Wallach, see footnote 17, pg 20; and Allman, see footnote 37.

42. Mary Anne Weaver, *New Yorker*, 16 May 1994.

43. Yuval Arnon Ohana, *Fellaheen in the Arab Revolt in Palestine 1936–39* (Hebrew), Machon Shiloah, Tel Aviv University, 1978. pg 133.

44. In a conversation with the author.

4: FROM ARABS TO PALESTINIANS

45. *Al-Hawadeth*, Lebanon, 5 January 1981.

46. For instance in a conversation with Raymond Edde in Lebanon, according to *Al-Nahar*, Beirut, 24 April 1973.

47. *Abu Iyad: Without a Homeland*, talks with Eric Rouleau, Misras (Hebrew) Jerusalem, 1979, pg 207. (The American edition of 1981 is titled *My Home, My Land: A Narrative of Palestinian Struggle.*)

48. Ya'ari, see footnote 20, pg 180.

49. For instance in my interview with him in summer 1993.

50. The translation is by Shefi Gabai, *Ma'ariv,* 3 February 1992.

51. *Al-Nahar*, Beirut, 31 December 1974.

52. *L'Europeo*, summer 1970.

53. Ya'ari, see footnote 20, pg 135.

54. *Al-Nahar*, 31 December 1974.

55. Hart, see footnote 2, pg 77.

56. In a conversation with the author in Jerusalem, 1990.

57. Destroyed in April 1948 by military units of the dissident Israel Freedom Fighters (Lehi, commonly known as the Stern Gang), and the Irgun Tsvai Leumi (Etsel), led by Menahem Begin.

58. Ya'ari, see footnote 20, pg 119.

59. The initials of "The Movement for the Liberation of Palestine" in Arabic mean "death." Accordingly the order of the letters was reversed and became the word "conquest."

60. Abu Iyad, see footnote 47, pg 86.

61. In the wake of rivalry between the Arab states in the early 1960s, Egypt under the leadership of Gamal Abdel Nasser initiated the establishment of an organization representing all the Palestinians. Headed by a veteran Palestinian official called Ahmed Shukairy, it was set up in 1964. Most of the Palestinians welcomed its establishment but in some of the Arab states, particularly Jordan, the new PLO organization was viewed with suspicion since it was seen as an instrument for Egyptian subversion and control of the Arab world. Arafat and his early Fatah people also had reservations about the PLO and its leader. When the Fatah called in 1964 to start an "armed struggle" against Israel, Shukairy attacked them bitterly. After the 1967 war, Arafat and Fatah joined the PLO framework, took over the organization and changed some of its basic principles. Thus it would embrace all those Palestinian groups calling for a military struggle against Israel. Arafat was elected Chairman of the organization.

62. Abu Iyad, see footnote 20, pg 65.

63. Ya'ari, see footnote 20, pg 45.

5: TURNING POINT

64. The National Water Carrier was part of Israel's central water project, the establishment of which started in the 1950s. It aimed to bring water from Galilee and the north, which enjoyed plentiful rainfall, to the arid south. It included a channel, mainly open, for water to flow from the Sea of Galilee (Lake Kinneret) in Galilee, to the Negev.

65. Ya'ari, footnote 20, pg 75.

66. Abu Iyad, see footnote 47, pg 77.

67. Ibid, pg 78.

68. Wallach, see footnote 17, pg 29.

69. He usually mentions Stalingrad, but in Gowers and Walker (see footnote 9) Arafat refers to a second Leningrad.

70. Gowers and Walker, see footnote 9, pg 73.

71. Ya'ari, see footnote 20, pg 97.

72. Ibid, pg 200.

73. Meeting with Egyptian journalists, 29 October 1985. Similar language is found in an interview in *Sawt al-Sha'ab* in Amman, 16 July 1983, and in a meeting with journalists in Tunis, 14 July 1983.

74. My interview with Arafat, summer 1993. Also the following paragraph.

6: HOMELAND IN A SUITCASE

75. Rashida Mahran, see footnote 2.

76. *Vanity Fair*, see footnote 37.

77. The journalists Janet and John Wallach, see footnote 17.

78. T. D. Allman, *Vanity Fair*, see footnote 37.

79. Ghassan Kanafani, the greatest Palestinian writer, born in Acre, was uprooted with his family in 1948. Joined the PFLP in Lebanon. Was murdered by Israeli agents when a car bomb exploded in Beirut in 1972.

80. Abu Iyad, see footnote 47, pg 72.

81. *New Yorker*, see footnote 42.

7: SURVIVAL

82. Fawaz Turki.

83. The survey was written by the author Mustafa Bakri according to *Ma'ariv*, 10 September 1993.

84. Dan Avidan in *Davar*, 8 November 1985.

85. In a conversation I held with their leader, Henry Sigman.

86. Interview in *Al-Sayyad*, Lebanon, 12 January 1975.

87. *Vanity Fair*, see footnote 37.

88. *L'Express* writer Alain Louyot.

89. *New Yorker*, see footnote 42.

90. The law was annulled in 1992. The Israeli peace activist Abie Nathan was found guilty and sentenced to a prison term on this account.

91. Menahem Klein in a conversation with the author, autumn 1994.

8: ASCETIC IMAGE, STRANGE MARRIAGE

92. *New Yorker*, see footnote 42.

93. Ibid.

94. His assistant Akram Haniyeh, in a conversation with the author.

95. Thomas Kiernan, see footnote 2.

96. Ibid, pg 108.

97. Wallach, see footnote 17, pg 58.

98. Ibid, pg 56.

99. For instance to the journalist Oriana Fallaci, see footnote 1.

100. In Ehud Ya'ari's book from 1969, see footnote 20.

101. Gowers and Walker, see footnote 9, pg 198.

102. The translation by Shefi Gabai, *Ma'ariv,* 3 February 1992.

103. Chapter 5, *Al-Rai al-Am,* Kuwait, 21 January 1987.

104. Rashida Mahran as above, and also the following quotation.

105. In view of this, there are some in the PLO leadership who are certain that this was not a real romance.

106. Raymonda Tawil's book *My Home, My Prison,* published by Adam Books, Tel Aviv, 1979.

107. The source of most of the details in this connection is an article in *New Yorker,* see footnote 42, and also several interviews with them which appeared in Arab newspapers published in London. Also conversations with Arafat's associates.

108. The first information about this was published in the Hebrew newspaper *Ha'aretz* by Gideon Levi.

109. The version also appears in Smadar Peri's article in *Yediot Ahronot,* 9 November 1992.

110. *New Yorker,* see footnote 42.

9: WAITING FOR THE CHAIRMAN

111. Afif Safieh called him this, Gowers and Walker, see footnote 9.

112. Ibid, pg 25.

113. The book is in Arabic, Modern Press Algiers, 1992.

114. In a conversation with the author, summer 1994.

115. Published in the French paper *Libération,* 22 November 1994.

116. Abu Iyad, see footnote 47, pg 234.

117. Ibid, 289.

118. Gowers and Walker, see footnote 9, pg 90.

119. During his first visit to Jericho, summer 1994. Quotes according to recollections of one of the participants in the meeting.

120. For instance Oded Granot, *Ma'ariv,* 16 September 1994, who calls his HQ a "Byzantine court."

121. Wallach, see footnote 17, pg 25.

122. Ibid pg 232.

123. Gowers and Walker, footnote 9, pg 55. According to Farouk Kaddoumi.

124. Ibid, pg 60.

125. *New Yorker,* see footnote 42.

10: RIDDLE AND SOLUTION

126. For example in his message of greeting to the Pope, December 1994.

127. Hart, see footnote 2, pg 439.

128. For example in an interview in the Hebrew newspaper *Al-Hamishmar*, 19 May 1993.

129. *Der Spiegel*, 30 December 1987.

130. Ibid, 30 December 1987.

131. Yehoshafat Harkabi "Arafat's achievements are permanent," Jerusalem, 3 June 1992.

132. To the quarterly *Middle East*, 13 May 1983.

11: FADING MYTH

133. For instance, the view of Iyad Sharraj, a psychiatrist and public personality in Gaza, who was an Arafat sympathizer and activist, according to Naomi Levitzky, *Yediot Ahronot,* 4 November 1994.

134. *Al-Quds,* end of October 1994.

135. Harkabi, see footnote 131.

136. *The Progressive,* see footnote 15.

137. Restrictions mainly through bans and distribution limitations in Gaza, November–December 1994.

138. The reference is to students' councils, workers' committees, youth organizations, research institutions, etc. See Emile Sahliyeh's book *In Search of Leadership:West Bank Politics since 1967,* Brookings Institute, Washington, D.C. 1988.

139. For instance to Janet and John Wallach, see footnote 17, pg 20.

140. Edward Said, see footnote 16. Michael Kelly, *New York Times* November 1994.

A NOTE ON THE AUTHOR

DANNY RUBINSTEIN is a columnist for the Hebrew daily
Ha'aretz and has been writing on Palestinian issues since 1967.
In 1988 he received the Sokolow Prize, Israel's equivalent of
the Pulitzer, for his reporting. He is the author of *The People of
Nowhere*, a book on the Palestinian vision of homeland. He
teaches in the department of Middle East History at Ben-Gurion University in Beersheva, and lives in Jerusalem.

A NOTE ON THE BOOK

This book was composed by Steerforth Press using a digital
version of Bembo, a typeface produced by Monotype in 1929
and based on the designs of Francesco Griffo, Venice, 1499. The
book was printed on acid free papers and bound by Quebecor
Printing ~ Book Press Inc. of North Brattleboro, Vermont.